How to Study

And Other Skills for Success in College

How to Study

And Other Skills for Success in College

Fifth Edition

Allan Mundsack

James Deese

Ellin K. Deese

McGraw-Hill

New York   Chicago   San Francisco   Lisbon   London   Madrid
Mexico City   Milan   New Delhi   San Juan   Seoul
Singapore   Sydney   Toronto

Contents

Preface

Studying is not a naturally occurring skill. Studying is an art that has to be learned, practiced, and refined. Even students who want to learn and who are eager to do well in college don't always know what to do or how to begin. They may not know how much to study or how to use their time wisely. It may not have occurred to them that different study techniques should be used for different subjects. Many students don't know how to use their textbooks efficiently, particularly the kinds of textbooks encountered in college. They don't know how to make the connection between the textbook and the lectures or how to absorb and retain the information. Many are not prepared for the lecture style of teaching at all.

Furthermore, many potentially good students are deficient in some basic skills; they may not be able to read well enough for college-level material; they may not be able to apply appropriate mathematical skills; they may have only a vague notion of English grammar. Too many students have trouble putting their ideas into words so that other people can understand them.

The majority of students come to a university with fears (and sometimes actual phobias) about mathematics and science. Not only are they deficient in knowledge in these subjects, but also they actively avoid taking the classes they need in these areas until the last year of their college career. This approach causes a great deal of anxiety at a time when the focus should be on the future.

Still others have sufficient preparation and are good at studying but don't know how to use all the resources available at the college. They can't use the library and the Internet efficiently; they never talk to a counselor; they don't realize that health services are available. They don't know how to keep personal problems separate from their academic work. After perhaps moving away from home for the first time, they don't know how to form a circle of mutually supportive friends.

This book is intended for all these students. It is for students still in high school intending to go to college. It is for community college students with anxiety about their transfer to a 4-year school. Older students returning to school after several years away from academia will find this book helpful. Even those who have not really thought about college yet may find motivation to continue their education in this book. And all who pick up this book and apply its techniques will begin to develop their own style and study process, the first and essential step to success in higher education.

Through the years, students and colleges change; a new edition of *How to Study* was due. To meet these changes, we have updated, expanded, and added various sections drawing on advice from students and colleagues. I offer particular thanks to my friends and colleagues Dr. Larry Andre and Larry Small for suggestions and critiques that were invaluable.

ALLAN MUNDSACK

To the Student

Why should you read this book? For one reason, you might learn something you don't already know. It may give you a reason to consider again those skills that you already have so that you might improve them. Skills you have, skills you want to improve, as well as skills you never thought about are discussed in this book.

To put it simply, this book is for you as a college student or soon-to-be college student. The trouble with books for students is that there are a lot of students, and students are all different. Keep that in mind as you read through this book. Look for those things for which you can say, "Yeah, that's my problem, all right." At the same time, although you may *think* you don't have a problem using the library, organizing your time, or balancing your social life and schoolwork, there may be tidbits in this book that may help you to improve those areas as well.

Don't overdo it; sometimes it's better just to sit back, absorb, and enjoy what you are reading. However, when you read a book titled *How to Study*, you can be sure that it has information that you can put to good use, and you should try to put into action the things you learn from this book. You will find all sorts of suggestions for dealing with all types of problems. Use this book to set yourself on the right track or to help to get yourself out of a hole if you think you're in one.

Good luck in your college experience.

About The Authors

Allan Mundsack, M.A., is on the mathematics faculty at Los Angeles Pierce College. He was twice elected President of the Academic Senate at Los Angeles Mission College, where he was vice-chairman of the mathematics department.

James Deese was Hugh Scott Hamilton Professor Emeritus of Psychology at the University of Virginia

Ellin K. Deese was former Assistant Dean in the College of Arts and Sciences and Associate Professor in the General Faculty and Lecturer in Religious Studies at the University of Virginia.

How to Study

And Other Skills for Success in College

Getting Off to a Good Start

WHY GO TO COLLEGE?

People go to college for many different reasons:

- To fulfill their parents' expectations.
- To do what all their friends are doing.
- To avoid getting a job.
- To increase earning power.
- To pursue a career that requires a college degree.
- To achieve personal fulfillment.
- To be an athlete.
- To experience the thrill of intellectual accomplishment.

However, the best reason of all to go to college is that you want to go. If this is your motive for going to college, then you will not drift through your years there, attending classes or skipping them as you please, reading only what cannot be avoided, looking only for the "easy A" courses, and never being touched or changed in any important way. Those who approach college life in a lackadaisical manner will find no satisfaction, yet, because of parental or peer pressure, they stay on.

1

To put it bluntly, unless you are willing to make your college years count, you might be better off doing something else. Not everyone should attend college, nor should everyone who does attend begin right after high school. Many college students profit greatly from taking a year or so off. A year or two out in the world helps some people sort out their priorities and goals. But regardless of whether you head to college right after high school or if you take a year or two off, it should be your own desire to learn and expand your horizons that brings you to class. That is the essential first ingredient to a successful college experience.

EVALUATING YOUR PRIORITIES

Think about your own situation. You may be in high school trying to decide whether or not to go to college. Perhaps you have been working for a while and think that you might want to enter college or return to get your degree. You may already be in college and, for one reason or another, are wondering whether you should stick it out just to get that degree.

A college degree is a kind of union card; you've got to have one to be accepted in many professions. But there are many good high-paying occupations that don't require a college degree. What is more, people often develop an interest in books, ideas, and intellectual pursuits after they have been out of school for a while. Recent statistics at my college, a typical urban college, indicate that the median age of college students has climbed into the high twenties.

Frequently, we are sad to say, high school is not the place that fosters intellectual interest. Take Bill. He finished high school with satisfactory grades and very high SAT scores. He would have been a good prospect for any selective college. But he knew at that point that he was not interested in learning from books. He liked working with his hands, and he liked being outdoors. His father was a well-known doctor, so you can imagine what pressure Bill was under to go to college. But he withstood the pressure and got himself a construction job. Bill discovered that he had a real talent for carpentry and began doing freelance cabinetry work, and he was great at it. After 5 years he found himself developing an interest in science. The kinds of books that once bored him in high school now fascinated him. He bought books on physics, the weather, and chemistry. By the time he applied to college at age 23, his goals were clear. He spent 4 happy and productive years as an undergraduate, supporting himself with loans, money from his family, and from the carpentry jobs he could pick up. He graduated with honors, and he ended up doing top-notch work in the medical school where his father had gone. For Bill, taking a break from academic education was a good thing to do.

One of the things Bill did during his last year of high school was to think a lot about what he was interested in. Many students need to do that but, in addition, they need to take stock of their abilities. College requires abilities that are sometimes not touched upon in high school. It can be a real shock to discover that high school math and college-level math are as different as a country road and a freeway.

Rating Your Abilities

Students often overrate themselves on the traits and abilities that contribute to success in college. One of the most important things you can do is make an *honest* appraisal of your strengths and weaknesses. You will find a table on page 4 that you can use to rate some of your traits and abilities. Check where you honestly think you stand on the issues listed. Discuss your ratings with people who really know you well—family, friends, counselors, and teachers—and try to decide where you have overestimated or underestimated yourself.

What You Can Learn from Your Standardized Test Scores

Standardized tests can help you gain some perspective about your academic standing. The people who take a test are the ones who establish the norms. For example, suppose you scored in the ninetieth percentile on a test given to high school seniors. That means that you scored better than 90 percent of the students who took the test. Remember, however, that not all high school seniors go to college. For those students who do, you may have scored at only the fiftieth percentile. Furthermore, because some colleges are more selective than others, you might find that your score puts you in the thirtieth percentile of the students at your school. Your score on a standardized test is meaningful only within the group of which you are a part.

The importance of standardized test results should not carry too much weight as you make decisions concerning your education. It has been shown that coaching can influence scores on such tests. Several companies have devoted themselves to providing a coaching service. Usually, your college's counseling services or your high school counselors can help you evaluate your test scores. Nearly every college has a counseling center for interviewing, testing, and counseling students about their academic and personal prob-

Self-Rating of Traits and Abilities

In the spaces below, check where you honestly think you stand on the traits and abilities listed. After you have done that, discuss your ratings with some other people who know you really well—students, friends, parents, counselors—and who might show you where you have overestimated or underestimated yourself.

In my school, I think I am in the—

Upper Fifth	Middle Three-Fifths	Lower Fifth	
			in speed of reading textbooks
			in ability to understand textbooks
			in ability to take notes
			in general preparation for college
			in amount of time I study
			in not wasting time
			in work habits
			in vocabulary (words I know and use)
			in grammar and punctuation
			in spelling
			in mathematical skills

lems. Trained counselors know not only how to give and interpret tests but also how to put together a total picture of your academic and personal qualifications. Tests are not infallible, and they need to be interpreted. Some of that you can do on your own (after all, you are the person who took the test), but counselors can help.

How Motivated Are You?

One of the things we have learned over the years is this: The biggest difference between those who barely get by in college and those who get top grades is motivation. We're not sure that this book will help you become motivated, but it should help you sort out the reasons you are not enthusiastic enough about your studies to do well.

Are You Prepared for the Competition?

Some high schools are good at preparing their students for the level of academic work required at college, and some are not. Yet whatever the quality of your high school and however great your achievements may be, you may not be prepared for the competition you'll find. This is what every college admissions officer knows—some students who have been at the top of the class in high school are going to have trouble in college, and some students who were real goof-offs in high school can make the grade in college. But making the grade takes work. College professors have different expectations from those of high school teachers. While they can be friendly and helpful, they are often not "student-friendly," as one student put it. They expect that you are going to do a lot on your own. There is more about this in a later chapter.

Examining Alternatives

Going to college and staying in college once you get there are not your only alternatives. You can enter the job market right after high school. Vocational school is a good choice for a person who is good at a trade and likes to do it. Postponing college for a time is a real alternative. Even jobs that are temporary and not particularly interesting can help you develop personal maturity. After a year or two of work, many students find that they are greatly motivated to study, and they appreciate college much more than they would have if they had gone there directly from high school. If you are in college and feel that you are only marking time, see your dean or adviser about taking a leave of absence. Most colleges are pretty flexible about leaves of absence.

You or your parents may be upset about any departure from the traditional sequence of high school, college, and then perhaps graduate school or professional school. Many people think of this as preparation for life and that we should get through it as quickly as possible. But we don't just prepare for life; we live it. We live it from the moment we are born until the day we die. The trick is to live it well—responsibly, productively, happily, meaningfully. All people are different; we don't develop at the same rate. Some experiences are wasted at one stage of our life, but the same experiences can be meaningful and important at another stage. If college is right for you now, fine. If not, postpone or interrupt your education, or find out what you can do to make it better. In the next few pages we tell you about some of the things that might help to make it better for you.

WHAT TO EXPECT

There are more than 2600 colleges and universities in the United States, and no two are exactly alike. Some are mainly for local students; others are for people across the country or even from around the world. Some have fewer than 1000 students, and there are some with nearly 50,000 students. Some are private, and some are public; some have a strong religious orientation; and some, both public and private, make a point of being secular. Some have a 2-year program, some have a 4-year undergraduate program, and some have affiliated graduate and professional schools. Some will take any high school graduate, while others are hard to get into.

If you are still facing a choice of a college or if you want to transfer, you might consult one of the books that details almost every U.S. college. You can find these books in most bookstores or in the library, and they are brought up to date every year. College counselors use them, and you and your parents can, too. These books contain information about costs, programs, size, and even whether or not the school offers the kind of social life you want. Whatever your decision is or has been, you should remember that no institution is perfect. You may think of your choice of a college as the most advantageous compromise. Problems that you may have had in high school aren't going to disappear just because you are in college.

LIVING ARRANGEMENTS

Living at Home

Most students go to a local college, and, even though some of these colleges have dormitories, many students live at home. This kind of arrangement has its advantages. It is cheaper, and you are in comfortable and familiar surroundings. It means that you will get the kind of home cooking you are used to instead of what—even at its best—is institutional food. Even though you may be living at home, you must try to establish the same kind of independence you would enjoy if you lived away from home. Rules that seemed appropriate when you were in high school don't necessarily apply. Negotiate respectfully with your parents to try to gain some independence, but remember that it is their house. If you meet some reluctance on your parents' part to negotiate a new set of rules, you may have to show that you have the maturity and responsibility to go with the new rules. If, however, there is too much friction at home or too little room, you should consider sharing an apartment with some friends.

If you live at home and commute, you need to go out of your way to get involved in the life of the college. That requires a certain amount of initiative. In all colleges, whether commuter or residential, students don't seek out one another nearly enough. They tend to form "safe" groups early on, gravitating to tables in the school cafeteria where they feel they will be immediately accepted. One of the goals of college life is to break these comfortable patterns of association. Branch out; seek to make the acquaintance of students who are serious about school and who have interests similar to yours. Join clubs on campus; go to concerts and sporting events. Make the first step; don't wait for somebody to seek you out.

Living in a Dormitory

If you attend a college far away from home, the odds are that you will spend at least the first year in a dormitory. Some people think dormitory life is great; some will hate it. Not all dormitories are alike, however. Some consist of suites of four or five rooms with a common living room, while others are made up of individual rooms, usually shared by two students, opening onto a corridor. Some are apartments for four to six people, often in a high-rise building. But most often you will have to share; you will have one or more roommates. Students who have their own room at home and are used to privacy may find it difficult to live with roommates. Frequently, colleges try to match people with similar interests and values, but they don't always succeed. Look upon the task of getting along with your roommate as one of the learning experiences offered by your college. Learn to give and take.

Many roommates, even when randomly matched, become close friends, and most get along well enough to survive the year. But sometimes they really can't stand each other. If you are stuck with a roommate you despise, try to solve the problem between yourselves. Often your roommate doesn't even realize what it is that bothers you. Be prepared to hear some things that you are doing that antagonize your roommate as well. Be as pleasant and unemotional as possible in bringing the grievances out into the open. Try to work out some sort of compromise. Be reasonable. If the problem persists, a resident staff member, typically someone from the junior or senior class or a graduate student, may be able to help. If things are really bad, you may have to try to change roommates.

Dormitory living also offers tempting distractions. There is nearly always something interesting going on, and it is easy to put off studying in favor of a card game, a chat session, computer games, or even watching your favorite sitcom. If you can resist these temptations when you have work to do, you will have conquered the major enemy in your pursuit of a successful college career.

Most colleges now give you a choice between coeducational and single-sex dormitories. Typically, the relationships between men and women in coeducational dormitories are that of being good friends. Pairing off is the exception rather than the rule, and dating is usually with persons living elsewhere.

Most schools have rules against alcohol and drugs in dormitories, but these rules are often broken. It is your decision to drink or use drugs, but you should know that students who regularly drink or spend a lot of time stoned *always* end up in academic trouble. Don't be tempted to abandon your personal values. Lifestyles differ, but you will certainly find people on campus who share your values and with whom you will be comfortable.

Dormitory living or living in shared apartments gives you a chance to get to know many different kinds of people. Take advantage of that—let it be a learning experience.

ORIENTATION AND ADVISING

Every college has some sort of orientation program for entering students, whether they are freshmen or transferring students. Even if the speakers are boring and repetitive, don't skip any part of this program if you can help it. You might miss out on some crucial information (about drop dates, for example), but, even more importantly, you'd be passing up a chance to meet a broad range of your classmates. Everyone feels lost and intimidated, and it is easy to strike up conversations with other students by commiserating with them about your mutual miseries.

You will be given a lot of miscellaneous printed material. Read it and save it because later in the year you will have questions that don't occur to you at first, and the handouts are your first line of information. It is in a sense a contract with the college. If you have questions that the handouts don't answer, go to official sources—resident staff, faculty advisers, and deans—rather than relying on guesses from the student grapevine.

Usually you are given a tour of the campus during orientation. Get to know the layout and the surrounding student community. You will feel at home sooner when you know something about the place where you will be living. Check out the library. You will—or should be—spending a lot of time there. Find out what computer facilities are available. Most colleges will provide you with Internet access and an e-mail account. The sooner you get familiar with the academic services available, the more efficient you will be as a student. Also check out the student union, if there is one. On most campuses this is the center of student activities. Wander through the classroom buildings; find your classrooms. Time yourself as you go from room to room. Determine how much time you will need to leave the place you live in order to get to class on time. On big campuses, it is easy to underestimate times of travel before the crush of students hits. Leave yourself ample time for travel. Do not be late for class, ever.

The student newspaper probably puts out an orientation issue. It will have a lot of useful information. Most students read the campus newspaper regularly. The newspaper contains listings for concerts, films, plays, etc. Usually during orientation there will be many things going on—parties, meetings, etc. Go to as many of these as you can. It will help you get over homesickness, and you will meet a lot of new people.

Placement tests in such subjects as mathematics, English, and foreign languages are usually given during the orientation period. Find out what tests you are required to take and which ones are not required but that would be advantageous for you to take. If you're still in high school and have taken some advanced placement courses, be sure to take the Advanced Placement Tests. If you score high enough, you may find yourself exempt from some courses and ahead on credits.

LEARNING TO COPE

Academic Demands

You have no doubt heard many times that "high school is not college." If your high school falls in the statistically average range, many of your classmates are not headed to college. You could easily stand out in comparison to your classmates. And if you went to a below-average high school, you could almost count on being in the upper half or even near the top of your class. In either case, you're likely to be in for a rude surprise. In most colleges, particularly four-year colleges, you are going to find yourself in the fast lane. Most college students were in the upper half of their high school class, and if they were lucky enough to go to a really good school, they've got a real advantage. Most college students are going to be people who were also student leaders—class officers, student body presidents, newspaper editors—in short, doers and achievers, some of them from the most prestigious high schools in the country.

What is more important, college professors are not likely to gear the work to the average student in their classes. A well-known professor, who is now retired, used to say that if more than two students understood what he was talking about, then he wasn't doing his job. Professors like to aim their courses at the superior students and expect everyone to meet higher standards. The same effort that got you As and Bs in high school could very well earn you Cs, Ds, or even Fs in college. You must be prepared to work harder for each class.

Because many students aren't prepared for the tougher job of studying in college, they do badly in their first semester. They get discouraged, and they want to drop out. That's why we think this book is especially useful to students entering college. We hope that it will help you head off trouble. Remember that many students who drop out are just as able and motivated as those who finish; they just weren't warned.

Aside from the competition and the higher standards of work, there's another big difference between high school and college. Even if you went to a high school that demanded a lot of work, it was pretty well laid out for you. Most of it was covered in class, and homework could sometimes be completed in class or in study hall. In high school there are fewer and less-demanding long-range projects such as term papers. You are graded mainly on what you did in class and in daily homework.

This is reversed in college. You spend relatively fewer hours in class, and except for labs, discussion sections, and seminars, you are hardly graded at all for what you do in class. Instead of an hour or two of homework for five classes, you should expect two or three hours of work for every hour spent in class. If you carry the standard load of 15 semester hours, you should easily expect to spend at least 30 hours a week in study and preparation. You should consider this to be your full-time job. There are no supervised study halls in which you have no choice but to work. Instead in college you will have to decide: Use all your nonclassroom time profitably or waste it. Your choice.

Most professors won't require you to do your work on a daily basis. You will be given a syllabus outlining an entire semester's work, and nobody checks to see if you are keeping up with the reading or working on your term papers. You might have an occasional quiz or midterm test; sometimes there will be only one exam, the final exam. Under these circumstances it is all too easy to let all the reading slide until the night before the final exam. This approach yields, at best, a C.

In college you are treated as an adult. Most of the selective colleges boast of this. You are on your own not only academically but also in how you behave. College life abounds with distractions that invite procrastination. In later chapters we deal with the problem of structuring your time so that you can get the most out of studying. But for now, let us remind you that with your new freedom goes a lot of responsibility.

Social Pressures

We all like to be liked, and everyone needs friends. Making and keeping friends will be one of the best things about your college years. But if you run into problems with your social life, your academic work will suffer.

Take Suzy, for example. A bright, hard-working student in the small town high school she attended, she was liked and respected by her high school classmates. Although she was not the most popular girl in her class, she had a few close friends both from school and from her church youth group. She looked forward to attending the state university. When she got to the university, she was placed in a dormitory whose residents all came from urban areas. They were more sophisticated than Suzy. All of them drank alcohol, two of them were experimenting with drugs, and most of them talked freely about their sexual experiences. Suzy had not encountered this sort of thing before. She felt awkward and uncomfortable. Her roommate, with no intention of being unkind, dubbed her the "country mouse," and one of the other girls changed this to the "church mouse." She couldn't feel close to anyone, and she became more and more the outsider. As she withdrew from social contacts, the other girls became increasingly hostile. Lacking the social skills and the confidence to seek friends elsewhere, Suzy spent most of her time alone. Although she studied diligently, it became harder and harder for her to concentrate. Most of the time she was depressed and anxious. She began to wonder if she was out of step with the rest of the world. By late October she was thoroughly miserable. After a long, tearful weekend at home, she withdrew from the university.

The saddest part of the story is that Suzy made no attempt to solve her personal problems. She might well have weathered the semester if she had sought the help of her resident adviser, her dean, or someone at the counseling center. The only thing she knew how to do was to control her environment by withdrawing to the safe, limited life that she knew.

There are all sorts of social pressures in college, many of them very different from the kinds of pressures you encounter in high school. You will be thrown in with people with different ideas, values, backgrounds, and lifestyles. Things that you had always taken for granted will be challenged. So your first year in college can be painful and threatening. Even if you go to a community college, you are going to find a far more diverse social environment than you experienced in high school. Many students will be older and perhaps hard for you to relate to. At the same time, remember, those students in their thirties (or older) are going to be equally challenged and threatened by students fresh out of high school.

If you find that your long-held values are being challenged, welcome the challenge as an opportunity to either solidify your values or alter them in the light of new information. Socrates said, "The unexamined life is not worth living for man." Don't be afraid to look at your life from a different perspective. It's one of the purposes of college—to provide an opportunity to explore ideas. You shouldn't claim an idea as your own unless you have examined it for yourself. The wider horizon of social life in college can help you do that. Be prepared for some uncomfortable moments. You may be the only person of your race, ethnicity, or religion, or you may be the only representative from your part of the country in your dormitory. If so, expect some of the other residents to be thoughtless. They may not mean to do so, but they may well offend you. Try to take such things in stride.

There are ways of dealing with social pressures in college without resorting to violence or giving up and continuing to be miserable. If you have trouble coping with social pressures, seek out the help of one of the support services at your institution.

Parental Pressure

Pressure sometimes comes from parents. Most parents mean well, but some of them really don't know how to help with the problems their sons or daughters have in adjusting to college. A few of them seem to go out of their way to add to their children's difficulties.

It is difficult for parents who are not living your life to know the kinds of problems you are facing. They don't know about the competition, both social and academic, that you face, and they may not be aware of the standards, both social and academic, to which you are held. If you are at an academically competitive college, the easy As and Bs that you were used to in high school may not be there. Your parents are bound to be disappointed if your college grades fall way below those you got in high school. They may bug you about trying harder. At worst they may threaten to take you out of college or cut off your funds. Weigh the fact that tuition, to say nothing of room and board, may be a real financial drain for your parents.

Sometimes parents regard their children as extensions of themselves and think that it's only right and natural that they control what their sons and daughters do. Sooner or later this has to stop, and the transition to college is a good place to bring it to a halt. At this point students are now adults and must be responsible for themselves (except for some financial considerations). Inevitably, students are going to do things that their parents regard as unacceptable. If you are confronted with a wall of anger and resentment because of something you do that does not fit with your parents' expectations, try to see the situation from their point of view. Try to work out a compromise. Sometimes a contrite "I'm sorry!" will do the trick. Keep in mind that resolving conflicts with parents is fundamentally different from resolving conflicts with friends and acquaintances. Parents love you. Unless you are able to sever the relationship completely, including the financial relationship, then you have a responsibility to work out some agreement. It always helps to try to understand how your parents feel. If you take care of the small things such as writing home, phoning occasionally, being responsible with money, doing your school work, and staying out of trouble with the law, then you have a basis for saying that you are acting responsibly, and a small infraction may be more easily forgiven. It is best to keep conflict to a minimum until you really are on your own. Typically, your family consists of the best friends you will ever have.

Another big source of conflict between parents and students is the choice of a major and the actual courses taken by the student. Some parents are convinced that only certain subjects are worth studying and that others are a waste of time. The engineer who can't understand why his son is taking courses in art and music, the artist who is horrified by his daughter's enthusiasm for economics and accounting, the physician who insists that his son follow a premedical curriculum, the lawyer who is upset because her daughter has no professional aspirations, and the mother who is shocked because her daughter wants to be an electrical engineer are all cases in point. Parents who have never been to college themselves have, perhaps, the most difficult time understanding your choices of courses and majors. But remember that students who merely accept the courses that their parents map out for them are usually headed for trouble. They are living out someone else's aspirations, not their own. Sometimes students get through college entirely on someone else's plans. Such people may discover when they are 35 or 40 that they really don't like what they are doing. Such scenarios are the makings of psychological problems and ulcers. It is important that your life's work be something *you* like to do so that you enjoy getting up in the morning and heading off to work. Few people are courageous enough to go back to school to correct the mistakes they made earlier.

College is the time for exploring alternatives, for examining life, for moving gradually and smoothly from parental direction to independence. At times it is hard for both students and parents. We hope that some parents will read this book and get the message we are sending. Resolving conflicts requires cooperation.

Financial Pressures

You may have had some experience in managing money before you get to college, but, somehow, it is different when you are on your own. You may be careless in budgeting your money and discover that no one is around to dole out cash when you run out. You'll save yourself a lot of money if you learn to manage your money effectively. College is expensive, and, if your parents are supporting you, you will do them a big favor by not being careless with money.

Students who go away to college frequently open a checking account in the town where their college is located. Parents will then deposit a certain amount of money into the account on a regular basis. Bank accounts are easily accessed through automated teller machines (ATMs) with debit cards. When you pay for purchases with a debit card, it is easy to lose sight of the fact that you are paying with money even though it doesn't look like money. When the monthly statement comes, it looks like money. It is very easy to overspend when it is so easy to spend. If you have never balanced a checkbook, get someone to show you how. Keeping accurate records is important. It can save you the embarrassment and considerable cost of a bounced check or a declined debit. Furthermore, don't write checks or use your debit card for every small item. Some banks charge you for each check you write and each time you use an ATM. So get in the habit of carrying enough cash for ordinary daily expenses such as school supplies or a snack, for example.

Expenses at the beginning of a college year are likely to be heavy because you will be buying books and supplies. After a few months, however, you will have a good idea about how much it costs you to live. If you don't get enough money from home, look for a part-time job. These are surprisingly easy to find in a college community. Having to pay part of your own expenses can have the effect of making you more motivated than those who do not. But then again, a part-time job forces a student to budget time more carefully. Management of time is the most important aspect of effective studying.

Many students receive financial aid from their college. A typical pattern is to have some funds in direct scholarship, some as a loan, and some in a work-study job. Every institution has a financial aid officer to whom a student can turn if it is necessary to have his or her aid package changed. In addition, many institutions have an emergency loan fund to help students out of temporary difficulties.

Sometimes commercial financial institutions will set up tables on many campuses offering students their first credit card. They are happy to give you an organizer or a calculator. "Establish your credit!" they say. "Everyone needs a credit card." No, you don't. These companies do indeed have legitimate credit cards, but their interest rates can be very high. The temptation is great to get a credit card, but, remember, you don't have a job. You are a student. Do you want to begin your working career with the obligation to repay student loans and huge credit card bills? There is plenty of time for credit cards after college.

Meet your financial obligations promptly. If you don't, you could damage your credit rating, and a bad credit rating will follow you for many years just when you are trying to establish yourself. Don't let your college bills go delinquent. If you are behind in paying your college bills or library and parking fines, you may be barred from the classroom. In any event, your college won't grant you a degree or send out transcripts until you have paid all your bills.

Being Involved

You probably know a good bit about college life by now. If you spend 15 hours a week in the classroom, 30 or so hours in study and review, and 56 hours sleeping, you are not far from the typical student. You still have about 60 hours left for other activities. Even if you have a job for 20 hours per week, you still have some time left. You can use that time to learn things that are not in the formal curriculum, such as how to work with and relate to other people. Organizations that interest you, intramural sports, exercise, discussion groups, and other recreational activities may fill this time. But don't overdo it; take it easy. Don't get too involved with too many extracurricular activities, particularly during the first few weeks. It may be harder than you think to settle into a routine that allows adequate time for study. You will need some time to assess just how hard college work will be for you. Take most of the first semester getting used to the academic schedule. Don't try to throw yourself into every activity that looks interesting or profitable.

Be sure to allow time for regular exercise: walking, jogging, weight training, aerobics, and so on are excellent for conditioning, and they have an unexpected side benefit. They are also antidotes for depression. When things are not going well in some class or other, it is easy to become depressed. A half-hour workout will tend to alleviate the depression and put your difficulties in a different perspective; things may not be as impossible as they seemed before the exercise.

If you play one of the varsity sports such as football or basketball, don't plan on participating in other extracurricular activities. Any sport will take up a lot of your time, and you will have to learn to budget your time even more carefully so that you will have time for study. Some big institutions run study sessions and tutoring services for varsity athletes. Make sure you take advantage of these or whatever other services your college offers to help you meet the time demands of playing on a varsity team.

Clubs and Organizations Every campus is crowded with clubs and organizations for every taste and interest. If drama isn't your thing, how about working at the campus radio station? Some schools even have a TV studio. There is always the student newspaper. There may be a debating society, a chess club, a folk dancing club, a ski club, a surfing club, or even a mountain climbing club, to mention just a few possibilities. Investigate those things that interest you. Find out what the people are like who are in organizations you might like to join.

There are a lot of reasons for choosing an organization to join. The most important one is to do something you like doing. Another is to give you experience at something you might want to do later in life or something related to your intended profession. If you are headed to medical school, you might want to join the drama club for fun and the premedical society because it sponsors activities that will help you meet your professional goals. And, of course, organizations provide opportunities for leadership and for learning how to work comfortably with other people.

A note of caution: Like varsity athletics, extracurricular activities place heavy demands on time. Putting out a newspaper is not a small job. You could find yourself giving so much time to your nonacademic activities that your grade point average will suffer. If you find yourself pressured by some extracurricular activity, drop out. No extracurricular activity is worth the risk of academic probation.

Student Government   Student government is a lot more important in college than it is in high school. On some campuses, students literally run everything but the academic curriculum. Student government may even be solely responsible for discipline. If you have a political streak or if you would like to have a say in how things are run, this is something to get into.

You will want to start at the local level. Go to your dorm council meetings or their equivalent (there are even such organizations for commuting students) and speak up. If you are active, there is a good chance you will get elected to some position sooner or later. That can give you an opportunity to test your skills at management and leadership. Again, remember not to spend too much time at it. Some people who are heavily into student government get swamped by it and neglect everything else.

Sororities and Fraternities   There are two basic types of fraternities and sororities—social and service. The intent of social sororities and fraternities is to provide a supportive network of friends on campus. Friendships formed while in college often last throughout life. On the other hand, the primary function of service sororities and fraternities is to serve the needs of the college or the community in some way.

Sororities and fraternities found at most 4-year colleges offer a way of life that is very attractive to many students. They provide opportunities for friendships and social activities with people who share your tastes and interests. On some campuses they are very important, and on others they are not. At some schools, the majority of students belong; at others, only 10 to 15 percent belong to a sorority or fraternity. Whether or not they are for you depends upon your needs and interests. Don't automatically assume that you should join one or, for that matter, that you should avoid them at all costs. For some people they are the most enjoyable part of their college years. For others they are narrow and confining. Don't be pressured one way or the other. If you participate in "rush" (the time during which sororities and fraternities actively recruit new members) the chances are that you will end up in one that suits you or not in one at all. If you do not pledge, it is probably for the best. It suggests that you most likely would not have been happy in any of the sororities or fraternities on your campus. If you end up in *any* organization that you don't like or that conflicts with your values and beliefs, drop out. If you drop out, the chances are good that you will find congenial friends elsewhere.

Do be involved in some aspect of college life. It will add immeasurably to the quality of your college experience. You will find that you are part of a living community and not merely an anonymous body in the classroom. And, of course, you will get back from an activity in proportion to what you put into it. If you give some of your time and energy to your college community, you will get something back in return.

Computers and Other Electronic Devices Every student will have a computer that is loaded not only with word processing and spreadsheet programs but also with *games*. You must look at your computer as a tool and not as your source of entertainment. The addictive nature of some of the games has been the downfall of many students. In the process of getting your education, you will find that attaining the next level in your favorite game is not as important as getting your paper written for class. If you know that you are addicted, you should bite the bullet and disable the games. Your computer is a tool.

Do not, under any circumstances, take your favorite music to class. Your professors will be offended that you find your music more important and interesting than the lectures. Also, when in class, turn off your cell phone.

Health Get acquainted with the health-care facilities on your campus. Know where to go to get help if you are injured or if you become ill. Know what preventive measures are available, from condoms to flu shots, and make use of them. Sometimes a bad case of the flu is enough to sink a semester. Do your part to maintain good health.

Now that we've covered some of the things that will help you get off to a good start in college, we're ready to get down to the main topic of this book: how to organize and use your time for effective study.

2

The Art of Studying

As we state in the Preface to this book, studying is an art form. You are not born knowing how to study. It is a skill that you must develop, practice, and refine. You may not be interested in some of your courses, or you may be interested but can't bring yourself to do the homework. People who aren't interested or who don't study as much as they should usually feel guilty. But that doesn't help. In fact it makes matters worse by adding anxiety and depression to the problem. Most people who advise students and who know what students' problems are believe that lack of motivation is responsible for more failures than inadequate background or lack of ability. Not being motivated is about the worst academic problem a student can face.

Before we tell you about some of the specific techniques of efficient study, we need to say something about the problem of motivation and what you can do about it. We can't make you want to learn, but we can say some things that might help you want to learn. First of all, you need to be clear about your reasons for going to college. On page 21, you will find a list of statements about motivation for college. There are no right, wrong, or magical answers. But if you are honest, you will be able to see yourself more clearly than if you don't think about such things. This kind of self-examination could lead you to change some of your goals or make you more aware of what you need to do in order to meet your goals.

IMPROVING MOTIVATION

Why is it hard to study? For one thing, there is the difference between high school and college. In high school someone is usually breathing down your neck every day to get you to do your work, and hardly any internal push is required. In college external pressure scarcely exists. You are on your own. For most students homework is not assigned on a regular basis, and sometimes a single assignment may be given for the entire semester.

Another reason it's hard to study has to do with the absence of short-term goals. Most students who go to college express some kind of career interest. They want to be doctors, lawyers, engineers, business executives, teachers, and so on. But these aims are often vague, and it is hard to see how day-to-day schoolwork relates to them. Few students are absolutely sure of what they want to do in life, and even fewer know exactly what they must do in college to prepare themselves for their chosen careers. If career aspirations should change, as they often do, students are adrift, and this causes insecurity and anxiety that make studying difficult.

One of the reasons for going to college is to determine a direction for your life. A college education should provide you with enough experience to help you find your career goal. There is nothing wrong with not knowing what you want to do, even after you've been in college for a while. Occupational choice is often difficult, particularly for students in a liberal arts program. In the absence of a firm career decision, many students find it difficult to work up much enthusiasm for studying. Or worse, they feel positively paralyzed without some clear goal in mind, even if they like their courses.

We can't do much in this kind of book to help you make your career decisions. This is something people must work out for themselves. Most campuses have career counseling services, and if you are concerned about your career goals, you should take advantage of these services. Career counseling can help you find out what your interests and talents really are, and they can provide information about the kinds of careers that attract people like you.

But if you don't feel any clear-cut calling to a particular occupation, don't let it worry you. One thing you can be sure of: If you haven't made a career choice by the time you are 21 or 22, the world will not come to an end. If you are in a liberal arts curriculum, remember that the subjects you study will

Motivation for College

The following statements are designed to help you think about your motivation and to give you some insight into it. Read completely through each group of items; then rank the items in importance by using 1 for the phrase that applies best to you, 2 for the phrase that applies next best, and so on.

I. I came (or will go) to college because—
_____ I know what I want to be, and college preparation is necessary for it.
_____ my folks wanted me to, even though I didn't.
_____ I thought it would be a lot of fun.
_____ I wanted to gain a better knowledge and understanding of the world I live in.
_____ many of my friends did, and I wanted to be with them.
_____ I wanted to get away from home.
_____ I am particularly interested in athletics and student activities.
_____ a college degree seems indispensable in this day and age.
_____ I like to study and am particularly interested in certain subjects.

II. I want to make grades that are good enough to—
_____ let me stay in college.
_____ meet degree requirements.
_____ let me participate in extracurricular activities.
_____ put me on the honor list and give me special recognition.

_____ make an outstanding record in college.

III. My motivation for making grades is to—
_____ prove to myself that I am learning something.
_____ secure a good job recommendation.
_____ please my family.
_____ do better than my competitors.
_____ live up to my reputation of being a good student.
_____ be respected by my teachers.

IV. I sometimes don't study when I should because—
_____ I worry about my personal problems.
_____ I simply can't get interested in certain subjects.
_____ I am too involved in extracurricular activities.
_____ I am bothered by illness and poor health.
_____ I get distracted by things going on around me.
_____ I tend to keep putting off my work.
_____ I am easily tempted to do more interesting things.

have little or no direct relation to what you will end up doing. The course of study is not designed to prepare you for any particular occupation. Rather its purpose is to make you a thoughtful person with skills in critical reading, thinking, or writing. In short, you will end up educated. Many employers want people who have a proven ability to learn, and they will teach you what they want you to know. It is our opinion that education, by definition, is valuable, and you should make the most of it.

The Importance of Grades

Grades are not the measure of a person, nor are they the sole measure of academic accomplishment. They are only one rather imperfect reflection of how much you have learned in your various courses. People can learn a great deal and acquire a good education without making high grades, and some students who make straight As may concentrate so much on getting them that they miss their education. Whether we like it or not, grades are one of things that society uses to judge what you are likely to accomplish in the future. However imperfect they may be, they do work.

If you want to go on to graduate or professional school, grades are even more important than you think. The competition among applicants for law school, medical school, veterinary school, graduate business school, and most programs in graduate arts and sciences is formidable. Your college grades will probably be the most important factor in determining whether you are admitted or not (although letters of recommendation sometimes count even more—we have more to say about this later). Experienced admissions officers know that grades predict success in advanced work better than do test scores. Of course, a few people with the right connections or with a great record of achievement in extracurricular affairs will be admitted despite mediocre grades. But that happens less often than you think. The best graduate and professional schools have two to ten times as many applicants as they have spaces. They can afford to take only the best. In many fields, no one with lower than a B average is even considered, and some schools seldom admit anyone with less than an A− average. So, if you plan to go on to advanced studies, you can't afford to dismiss grades as unimportant, even if you have reservations about them, as many of us do.

Satisfaction in Study

Learning, even studying, doesn't have to be a chore. It can be a real source of satisfaction. In the last chapter we point out that if you see no intrinsic value in learning, perhaps you shouldn't be in college, at least for now. Part of the trick in liking to study is in knowing what to learn and how to learn it. If you can pick up a book, read it with reasonable speed, and know how to select the main points and remember them, you're the kind of person who probably does get satisfaction from learning. You're lucky. You will be the richer person for it. Besides acquiring some new information or being challenged to examine some new ideas, you'll have the kind of feeling of pride that a craftsperson has in work well done. Once you have done a good job at studying, you will be in a better position to do it again. The more you read and learn, the easier it is to read and learn. Instead of being a dull, frustrating chore, studying will be something satisfying in itself. If you develop a high level of skill in studying, we can almost guarantee that you will come to enjoy studying more and that you won't dread it. If, despite your best efforts, studying is still a dull task, it may be that you have a problem in reading, writing, or doing basic arithmetic. If so, do something about it. Your college almost certainly has some program for helping students for whom the ordinary procedures in studying are a monumental chore.

Good study habits will let you get more done in less time. The time you save can be used for the things you like to do best—a reward for yourself. We are confident that if you learn to study as outlined in this book, you will have more time for the things you like to do, even if it's more studying. Evidence shows that students who have been taught how-to-study methods make better grades with less time spent in studying than those students who have not been instructed.

Of course, it is not *how much* you study but *how well*. Students who study all the time demonstrate that they are not studying effectively, and they frequently get poorer grades than many of those who study a shorter amount of time. Many bright students study day and night without getting the grades they ought to. As it is with many other things we do, it's the quality rather than the quantity that counts.

Study Groups

One of the surest means to success in your academic career is to create, maintain, and participate in study groups. Like-minded students working together can magnify their results in each class by picking one another's brains and by forming mutual reliance patterns.

Early in one semester a study group was formed consisting of five people who had several classes together. One evening one of the members of the group was in a terrible car accident. She was badly injured; many bones were broken, and the car's battery ended up on her chest with acid leaking onto her body. She spent the rest of the semester in the hospital recovering from her injuries.

The members of her study group obtained permission from the professors to tape-record the class sessions, went to her hospital room to play back the recordings, read the textbook to her, and discussed the lectures with the injured student. When the instructors heard of the effort put forth by the group, they agreed to go to the hospital room to administer exams. The result was that the injured student passed all her classes that semester, and 2 years later she graduated at the top of her class. This is a more tragic situation than you are likely to face in your school life, but it indicates what can happen with the help of a well-functioning study group.

It is important to select members for your study group carefully. Probably in the first semester at a new school you will not know anyone well, but within a week or two some people will strike you as being serious as well as friendly. Approach two or three such people and suggest that you meet once or twice a week for a mutually beneficial study group. Their willingness to participate is a good indicator of their seriousness.

Have a good place in mind to suggest to meet. This place should be convenient for everyone, comfortable, and free of distractions. Conference rooms are usually available in the library. Empty classrooms may be used, but be sure they are really empty for the time you intend to use them. Dormitory rooms may be the meeting places of last resort because they are usually full of distracting influences such as roommates, television, and music.

Try not to be bossy, but have some agenda prepared for the first meeting. A productive first meeting will tend to encourage continued participation by the other members. Someone must take the reins to ensure that the meeting does not disintegrate into a bull session. The best groups will make all the members feel that they have an investment in its success. Each person should be able to rely on each other person to participate fully, attend class, read the required material, and do the assignments.

The group must have the backbone to weed out those people who are mere hangers-on. The group cannot survive by dragging along people with no commitment to its success.

Don't let the meetings interfere with your own private study time. Study groups are to *supplement* your classroom experience. Make a schedule of individual study time as well as group time, and stick to it.

In subsequent semesters, you may want to continue the study groups if you share classes with the members. You will find that in the best of circumstances people will drop out and new ones will be added. Sometimes you will need to start over. Don't be afraid to create a new group if the old one isn't meeting your expectations.

Technology

A student in today's technological age certainly can complete a degree the old-fashioned way by using only paper for research and typewriters for written papers, but much more can be done more easily using computers for word processing, for access to the World Wide Web, computer algebra systems, and spreadsheets. It is probably unnecessary to say that any student entering college today must be computer-literate in order to compete on equal footing with other students. Even handheld calculators have graphing capabilities and built-in algebra systems. But none of these devices actually siphons knowledge into your brain. They are only tools that help information flow more easily and rapidly. The learning still takes place in your brain. There is no substitute for reading word for word the words of Wordsworth, for example. Your professors will make it clear what aspect of technology is required, permitted but not required, or forbidden. Because the professors usually have ways of checking to see whether or not the students are following the rules, be sure that you adhere closely to the rules.

Keeping an Open Mind

All students must cultivate an open mind. We all absorb aspects of our culture that to us seem correct and are not to be challenged. The vast majority of Americans believe strongly that democracy and capitalism are the proper political and economic systems. It is difficult for many people not to filter information about communism, for example, through their view of capitalism. Learning about communism does not make one a communist. Learning about witchcraft does not make one a witch. You must learn to separate knowledge from propaganda. If the phrase, "As an American, I . . ." for example, shows up in one of your papers, then that means that you are filtering the information being discussed through your concept of what an American typically believes and not accepting the information for what it is. Most professors are interested in what *you* think, not what society thinks; they want to know what *you* think, not what your religion teaches. It is sometimes very difficult to distinguish between your deeply held beliefs and a dispassionate view of information, but it is the mark of an educated person to be able to do it. It has been said that the educated mind can hold two opposite views at the same time. Be able to see two (or more) sides of an issue, and understand the arguments for each side. (This is the essence of a "compare and contrast" essay.)

All of this falls under the heading of an open mind. Be willing to hear a new idea—not necessarily to agree with it, but to understand it. Your college life should be filled with new ideas, and even the ones you reject help you to form your own philosophy of life.

Learning Modes

Some people learn visually, some by touch, some by hearing, and some by a combination of these senses. Joni could sit through a lecture and not get the main points, but if she took lots of notes as the professor spoke, the main points would become clear to her. The act of combining hearing, writing, and finally seeing the words allowed her to understand the main points of the lecture. Another person at the same lecture may take only a few notes because the main points were immediately clear just by listening to the professor. Another person may not see the main points until after reading the portion of the textbook on the same topic. Each individual has a primary mode of learning.

It is important to understand your primary mode of learning. Many students know by experience what they need to do in order to get the information, but many do not know why they struggle to understand what others seem to get easily. There are testing procedures that can pinpoint your particular mode of learning, and they can provide you with a prescription for the most efficient way for you to approach each class. If you struggle much more than your classmates, ask for an appointment with your counselor who can direct you to an appropriate testing center.

DEVELOPING PERSONAL EFFICIENCY

Sara is chronically behind in her work. It is not that she doesn't try. Every evening after supper she goes to her room and picks up a book. Most of the time, however, something happens to interrupt her. The telephone rings, or someone has an urgent personal problem that he or she wants to talk about, or she can't find the book she needs. By the time she gets down to work, she's too sleepy to concentrate.

Scott, a premed student, is so worried about his performance in chemistry that he spends 4 and 5 hours at a time studying it and neglects his other subjects. He doesn't think about them until exam time, when he realizes how far behind he is. Jack, on the other hand, is so anxious about falling behind that he jumps from one subject to another and never stays with one long enough to master the material.

Sara, Scott, and Jack share the same problem. They have not learned how to organize their time for effective study. Even if you're a student who studies long and hard, the chances are that you're wasting time. In fact, as we imply above, if you study many more hours than other people who have the same kind of schedule, you're probably wasting a good deal of time. This problem can be corrected, but only you can do it. The remedies we suggest have to be, like a diet, faithfully carried out.

The Value of a Schedule

The most important thing you can do by way of organizing your life for studying is to make a schedule. A schedule makes time by cutting out wasted motion. It keeps you from worrying about what you are supposed to be doing next. Most things in life are organized for you. If you have a job, you are supposed to show up at a particular time, and your meal times are pretty much set. But, in studying, you have to organize your own time.

And there are other benefits from organizing your time. Having time assigned for each task prevents you from neglecting one thing for another. It helps you to study subjects at the best time for those subjects rather than at the wrong time. By having a schedule, you can avoid the hit-or-miss approach that causes some students to tackle the hardest or dullest subject when they are least able to concentrate.

A Sample Schedule

We can't make a schedule for you. You have to make your own so that it fits your class hours, activities, and part-time work. We can, however, give you some tips on how to make one. Start with the sample on page 29. There you will find a schedule for a student carrying a fairly heavy load. She is taking economics, psychology, German, organic chemistry, and English. She also is in ROTC, and she holds a part-time job 10 hours a week. You will find blank schedules in the back of this book. Make copies to practice with until you have it right.

We have blocked out her schedule into 1-hour periods because many of the gaps in a student's schedule are only an hour long. These spare hours add up, and you should use them. Research on working effectively shows that most people do best by working intensely for a reasonable period of time and then resting or switching to another task. Trying to be brave and work hard for 3 hours straight usually results in headaches, frustration, poorly done work, and the need to redo much of the work. A 3-hour period should have at least three breaks of 5 to 10 minutes each. Do something different, even if it's staring at the inside of your eyelids for a time, stand up and stretch your legs, get something to drink or a snack. You will be able to work more efficiently, accurately, and happily after a short break. You should experiment at the beginning to find what work-break routine works best for you. Turn your cell phone off during study periods. Treat your schedule as you would a schedule at your job. (Your job right now is to be student.) There is more about this later, but an hour that is well used is pretty close to the best unit of time for most college study.

Notice that the hours in the sample are blocked off for specific subjects. Assigning time to specific subjects will save you the time you might spend trying to decide what to study next, and it will help you put together the right books and materials.

The sample schedule is tough. This student is serious—she wants to do well, but she is on the edge of overdoing it. She is very busy. You may not want to settle for so rigorous a routine, but make your schedule as close to your own ideal as you can. Remember, however, you're supposed to stick to your schedule. Don't make it so challenging that you won't follow it. A schedule that you won't follow is less than useless because it deludes you into thinking that you are doing something that you really aren't.

Put your schedule in a place where you are apt to look at it: in your notebook, over your desk, or even in the mirror or on your "must do" bulletin board.

Studying for Lecture Classes

This section addresses lecture classes such as history, sociology, psychology, and the like. There are two parts to studying for a lecture class: studying before the lecture and studying after the lecture. And maybe there is a third—studying before an exam.

You should have a notebook devoted to each lecture course. When you open your notebook, consider the pages as if they were numbered in a book; that is, the even-numbered pages are on the left, and the odd-numbered pages are on the right. To prepare for a lecture class, read the proposed material that will be included in the lecture. As you read, make notes of the main points on the left side of your open notebook, that is, on an even-numbered page.

Sample Schedule

Time \ Day	Monday	Tuesday	Wednesday	Thursday	Friday	Saturday	Sunday
7:00	← DRESS	AND	EAT →			↑	
8:00	ECON.	Study	ECON.	Study	Study		
8:30	LECT.	Engl.	LECT.	Engl.	German		
9:00	Study	ENGL.	Study	ENGL.	ECON.		
9:30	German	CLASS	German	CLASS	DISC.		
10:00	GERMAN	↓	GERMAN	↓	GERMAN		
10:30	CLASS	PSYCH.	CLASS	PSYCH.	CLASS		
11:00	Study	LECT.	Study	LECT.	Study		
11:30	Econ.	↓	Econ.	↓	Psych.		
12:00	←		LUNCH	→			
12:30			↓				
1:00	CHEM.	CHEM.	CHEM.	ROTC	CHEM.		
1:30	LECT.	LAB.	LECT.		LECT.		
2:00	Study		Study		Study		
2:30	Chem.		Chem.	↓	Chem.	Eight hours of	
3:00	Job		Job	Job	Job	study distributed	
3:30						as needed among	
4:00						five subjects	
4:30		↓		↓	↓		
5:00		Recre-		Recre-	Study		
5:30	↓	ation	↓	ation	German		
6:00	←		DINNER	→			
6:30			↓				
7:00	Study	Study	Study	Study	Recre-		
7:30	Engl.	Psych.	Engl.	Chem.	ation		
8:00	Study	Study	Library		Recre-		
8:30	Psych.	Econ.	(Papers	↓	ation		
9:00	Study	Study	or	Study	or		
9:30	Chem.	German	reports)	Econ.	Library		
10:00	←		RECREATION	→			
10:30			↓				
11:00	←		SLEEP	→			↓

Then, during the lecture itself, open the notebook to the corresponding page and make notes on the odd-numbered page side, highlighting in some way the items that appear on both the even- and odd-numbered pages. If there are items on the left side that are not mentioned in the lecture, they are probably not going to be on the exam. Your professor doesn't think they are particularly important. If the items appear on both sides, both you and the professor think they are important. They will likely appear on the exam. Those items that appear on the right side only are most likely the professor's favorite topics. These might be viewed as good essay question topics, and you should put some extra thought into them. If the lecture is a completely different topic from what you find in the textbook, don't hesitate to ask the instructor for reading material that does parallel the lecture. It is very helpful to get things from two sources, lectures and reading.

As soon after class as possible, review, highlight, and condense your notes using the ideas above. Keep all notes and revisions in the same notebook. If you let too much time pass before you do the revision of your notes, you'll find it to be a hopeless task. It's a sinking feeling to look at your notes and say to yourself, "Why did I write that down?" Before an exam, your review is easy because the revised notes are concise and to the point.

Studying for Lecture Classes in Science   In many science classes, it is difficult to read ahead, especially in the heavily math-dependent classes such as physics and chemistry. Prepare as you would for other lecture classes. But when the material gets too difficult in these classes, at least sort out the vocabulary words and write down the formulas that apply to the upcoming lecture. On the odd-numbered pages write down any definitions and examples of the use of the formulas that are given in the lecture.

Studying for Mathematics and Language Classes

In most beginning language classes, and in some mathematics classes, you have to recite in one form or another, either orally or in written form on a chalkboard. Try to prepare for these classes immediately before class, if possible. Even if you have only 15 minutes, use them to go over what you might have to say or write.

There is a fundamental difference between these classes and lecture classes. These classes are almost always cumulative. If you miss the discussion of, say, the Jackson administration in American History, you have missed a crucial episode. However, the chances are that you will be able to follow the events that led up to the Civil War. But in language and math classes, if you miss something early on, you will find yourself totally baffled by what comes up later. Poor preparation snowballs in such courses. And it gets worse. If you don't know what is going on, you feel like an idiot asking questions. So as assignments pile up, you fall farther and farther behind. The moral is: Keep up. But if you do fall behind, get help immediately. See your instructor, a tutor, your adviser, or members of your study group.

Making a Schedule

As we've said before, how you make your schedule is your own business, and a highly individual business it is. What you do depends upon your work habits, your abilities, and the courses you are taking. The old rule says that you should spend 2 hours in studying for every 1 hour of class. Maybe that's true; maybe not. It depends on the class and your relation to the subject matter. For some subjects you may need fewer than 2 hours; for others it may take more. You have to make an honest assessment of your abilities in a given class. Are you a slow reader? Can you work out problem sets but only after taking frequent breaks to relieve the tension? These are the kinds of things that you need to consider when you establish your schedule. Everybody—factory and office workers included—does a worse job when working very long hours than when working for reasonable periods. If you start out trying to do too much, you will get discouraged and perhaps give up altogether. If we have any realistic advice to give you about a study schedule, it is to be moderate and sensible. Know your limitations (more about this later) and your assets.

As soon as you know when your classes meet, put them in your schedule. *Don't do this at your preregistration;* do it when you are sure of your classes. Next, fill in the other regular activities you know about (job, ROTC, etc.). Now estimate how much time you'll need to do the work for each of your classes. Later you can adjust the study time to suit the way things are really shaping up. If you're a quick study in languages, you may shave time for French in order to make room for math and organic chemistry. On the other hand, if languages are an uphill struggle for you, then allow extra time for them.

You may want to compare your provisional schedule with the sample provided in this chapter. The student who made this schedule has allotted about 32 hours a week for studying, 22 hours of which are scheduled for particular subjects during the week, and about 10 of which are to be used as needed. In addition, she has reserved one evening a week for working in the library or in the computer lab on papers, reports, and so forth. She has kept another evening on reserve for emergencies. (Yes, you must plan your emergencies!) Remember, this student has a heavy load, and she must be an efficient user of her time. Should you be also?

Of the five courses she's taking, organic chemistry will take the most time. It has a laboratory, and that requires lab reports. It's the killer course for pre-meds, so the competition is tough, and even a passing grade is hard to get. With good sense, she has assigned 6 of her scheduled hours to chemistry, and she expects to spend some extra time on it during the weekend. Three of her scheduled study hours come right after the lecture classes. She has scheduled a fourth hour on Monday evening to prepare for the laboratory on Tuesday. The last two she's assigned to Thursday night in order to have a larger stretch of time to write up lab reports.

German is the most difficult of her remaining subjects. While she is moderately good at languages, her instructor has a reputation for being tough. In any language course there is a lot of memorizing and translating. So she has scheduled 5 hours for German. She has managed to schedule 3 of the hours just before the class so she can be prepared for recitation.

She has anticipated little trouble with economics. The course she is taking is in money and banking, something in which she has an interest. The course description includes the development of the banking system, and she has a good background in the Federal Reserve System from a history course she took. Moreover, the scuttlebutt on campus is that the professor teaching the course is an excellent lecturer who places the greater emphasis upon lecture material. She has scheduled 4 hours a week for economics, 2 of them after the lecture class and 1 on Thursday evening before the meeting of the discussion section on Friday.

She doesn't expect much trouble from her English lit course. She is a fast reader, and she has read some of the assigned readings before. Rereading these with an eye to putting them in the context created by the instructor will be fun. She needs, at this stage, only to keep up with the readings in order to be prepared for class. But she knows that she will have to find some extra time in the second half of the semester for this class when she will have to produce a major term paper.

This leaves psychology. It is a large lecture course with a lot of different kinds of students. The course, she thinks, will be interesting and probably easy. The course syllabus tells her that the main thing is to study the textbook; the lectures will mainly explain and illustrate it. But the textbook is a big one, and so she has scheduled 3 hours a week to study psychology, and she has reserved a couple of hours on the weekend in case she needs more time.

This schedule was her first guess as to the amount of time she would need to study. She knows that she might have underestimated the amount of work she will have to do. If this proves to be the case, she can use some of the free time on Friday evening for studying. If she is lucky enough to have one or more study groups, the Friday evening and weekend days would be a good time to schedule their meetings.

If you add up her assigned times, you will find that she will be in class or lab about 19 hours a week, studying about 32 hours a week, and working 9½ hours a week. No doubt about it, this is a heavy schedule, but this student is ambitious and disciplined, and she thinks that she can hold to it. There is more time left over than you might think. She can quit studying at 10 o'clock. That gives her an hour or so, depending on how much sleep she needs, for going to the local hangout, watching TV (she's a news freak), or just talking with friends. She has scheduled leisurely hours for meals. She has time for exercise, and most of the weekend is free. For at least part of the semester, she will be able to take off one or two evenings a week (Wednesday and Friday) in addition to Saturday. What she hasn't done is schedule time for student activities—meetings, dorm council, and so forth. She may have to make time for these things later on. Though her schedule is a rigorous one—it calls for more studying than most students do—it is still leisurely compared with the schedule of a doctor, lawyer, business executive, working mother, or someone who moonlights on a second job.

Blocking Out Your Study Time

In summary, here are our suggestions for blocking out your study time:

1. Assign less time to easier subjects, even those you like, and more time for those that are hard for you.

2. Spread out study time. People learn more and remember better when studying is spread out over several sessions rather than being crammed into one session.

3. As a general rule, schedule a study review session, particularly of class notes, as close as possible after the class. This way you can correct and add to your notes while the information is still fresh in your head. But, if your class is mainly recitation, as in a beginning foreign language, you should schedule a review period just *before* the class.

4. Before final exam time set up a special schedule. Also work into your schedule a plan for researching and writing term papers.

Revising a Schedule

Your first schedule for the semester should not be the last. You may have been unrealistic about your total study time—either underestimating or overestimating. If so, revise. Use the schedule as a guide, particularly if you don't do as well as you think you should. After you have settled down to a regular routine, you may revise your schedule to better suit your needs. Demands vary, and you will want to trade around study times now and then. The whole purpose of a schedule is to get you into regular work habits. If you establish good work habits, you won't need to rely on your schedule rigidly, and you will be able to use it only as a convenient reminder.

What if you are a total goof-off? We've known students who were stoned most of the time or spent most of the day in bed in their rooms. You are not likely to be that extreme, but if you think you have a serious problem in keeping to any sort of schedule, seek some help. The chances are that it isn't just that you are lazy or overwhelmed by a new life or all the socializing you've suddenly discovered. Rather it is probably something that you don't recognize yourself. Take advantage of the services provided by your dean, by counseling services, or by any other person or agency that you think you might be comfortable with. Putting off looking for help just makes the problem worse.

Using Time Effectively

Many students start out with a schedule but then abandon it because they can't seem to make it work. Take Pete, for example. His schedule called for him to read for English literature from seven until ten o'clock. With the best of intentions, he would sit down at his desk promptly at seven. On an all too typical day, he began to read, but when he reached for his pen to make notes, it wasn't where he thought he'd left it. It wasn't in his jacket pocket either, and he didn't find another one in his desk drawer. He went across the hall to borrow one from a friend, but a hot discussion on the prospects of the Washington Redskins took him in, and he forgot that he was supposed to be studying English. When he finally got around to leaving, somebody said something about a great TV show that was on at eight o'clock. Pete managed to persuade himself that he could study English during the commercials. But then he was daydreaming about the next weekend. Should he try to go home to borrow one of the family cars? Ten o'clock and time to go out for a beer, and there is still no work done.

Dribbling away time is the single biggest barrier to effective study. If this is a major problem for you, you need to seek help. There are several possibilities. One is an assigned study session. Many institutions have them. They are common in varsity athletic programs, but usually everyone is welcome, and in many places they have become standard. Campus ministries sometimes sponsor them. Another possibility is to seek some guidance. You may not be aware of the origin of your problem and having somebody to talk to who has had experience with a lot of similar cases may be just what you need. These are some practical measures you can take to help you use your study time more effectively.

Establish Definite Study Periods   When you establish a study period, make up your mind that during that time you'll *do nothing else but study*. Start by making your study periods short, interspersed with definite periods of rest or relaxation. Planning to study for 3 hours at a crack and then doing nothing is worse than useless; it makes you feel guilty and hopeless. Settle for 1 hour at a time. If you really have a problem concentrating, cut that down. Twenty minutes spent actually studying are better than an hour procrastinating. With a modest goal, you'll be more likely to do what you set out to do, and you will have the feeling that you have really done something. If you opt for a 20-minute study time, take a 10-minute break and them go back for another 20 minutes. If you can't concentrate for even such a short period of time, you're in trouble and need help. Something to consider is that you may not be ready for college. Dropping out for a year or two is better than amassing a lot of rotten grades.

Once you've gotten used to an easy schedule, gradually change it. The satisfaction that comes from working well when you work will help you reach for longer times. Even students who are very proficient at studying, however, should take periodic breaks in order to sustain their concentration.

Find a Good Place to Study   Some people can study in the middle of the year's biggest party, but most of us need a good place to do our work. The best place is to sit at a table or desk, not on a bed. If you read or study in a prone position, you're much more likely to daydream or doze off. Sitting up straight provides you with the muscle tone necessary to keep you alert.

If you are easily distracted, keep your table or desk clear of everything not connected with study. That means no pictures, trophies, or radios. For the same reason, a table or desk that faces a wall or at least away from people is a good idea.

Good lighting that covers the entire work area is important. Avoid strong shadows on your work. If it's hard to see part of your work, you'll tire more easily and give up more quickly. Strong light that is comfortable, pleasant, and evenly distributed will make your task easier. If you are working with a computer, you don't want a glare on the screen. Glare is a particularly serious problem if you are working with a backlit screen as is the case with laptops.

When you sit down to study, make sure that everything you need is at hand. Textbooks, notebooks, pens, pencils, computer disks, erasers, and a good dictionary are all included. Having to hunt for something not only wastes time but also invites distraction. Remember, Pete's wasted evening started with a missing pen.

Any place that provides the best combination of the conditions we describe is a good place to work. Your own room, if other people can't distract you, is a good place. Even if you have a roommate, your room can be a good place, provided that your roommate is willing to respect your privacy.

Of course, other people in your dormitory, fraternity, sorority, or apartment are on different schedules and are probably no more disciplined than you are. They interrupt you; they carry on interesting conversations within earshot; they listen to the radio or to music, or they watch TV. In the war against time dribbling away, our worst enemies can be our friends, family, and roommates.

So there will be times when you'll want to find a place to work where other people can't bother you. A good place is the library. Find an isolated spot facing away from the entrance. Libraries are usually pretty good about enforcing rules against talking and other kinds of distractions. There are no TVs and no pictures of boyfriends or girlfriends to look at. The atmosphere discourages daydreaming. Nobody should be surprised to learn that students who regularly study in the library make, on the average, better grades than those who do not.

Many students say that they don't like to study in the library. That may be because they are not really motivated to study. If you are worried that you may miss out on something at the dormitory, you may feel itchy at the library. The important thing is to find some place where you can concentrate on studying. Experiment if you have a problem here.

In some large institutions or places in which facilities are tight, the library may be too crowded. But in most places you can find a location that is free of distractions. Unused classrooms make good places to study. Then, some people who have learned to use their time well can study effectively in the most unusual places, on park benches, under shady trees, on buses (but watch out for motion sickness). But if you are learning the art of concentration, pick the library or some other place designed for and restricted to studying.

Many dormitories and fraternity and sorority houses as well as such places as student unions and campus ministry houses have special study rooms that are quiet and largely free of disturbances. These rooms make good substitutes for the library.

Improving Your Ability to Concentrate

No matter how well you organize your time or how good your place to study is, you will have to use your mind effectively in order to accomplish something. Many things can improve your ability to concentrate. Physical fitness is one of them. Eat regular meals and get enough sleep. Don't try to live it up and study at the same time. Drinking and some drugs such as marijuana and cocaine give you the feeling that you are really doing a great job, but nothing could be farther from the truth.

Of all of the enemies of concentration probably the most common is a lack of regular sleep. If you are away from home, it is very tempting to stay up until the early morning hours, even if it is only to watch late movies, and then sleep until eleven o'clock. Try to keep your sleeping hours on a reasonable schedule and get what is for you the right amount of sleep.

Keeping fit means both exercise and recreation. If you like tennis or racquetball, set aside regular times to play. Having a regular partner helps to keep to a schedule. You depend on each other to be there, and you more likely will be. If you are not into sports, then jogging, tossing a Frisbee around, or even regular walking can give you the kind of exercise you need.

Sleepiness is the curse of the college student. Of course you are going to be sleepy if you don't have regular hours of sleep during the night. But some students are sleepy in class anyway, and some fall asleep while they are trying to study. Study is a quiet activity, and sometimes it is boring. Don't yield to temptation to put off studying until you are fresh because doing so will only get you off your schedule. The best way to fight sleepiness is to take 5-minute breaks during which you rest or even nap (if you do nap, make sure you have a way of waking up). Most people snap back quickly after a short rest. Move

How Good a Student Are You?

Read carefully each of the following questions, and answer it honestly by writing a "yes" or "no" in the margin to the left of the question. When you are finished, see the directions for scoring at the bottom of the questions.

1. Can you think of anything that prevents you from doing your best work?
2. Do you usually study every day in the same place?
3. Do you usually know in the morning just how you are going to spend your day?
4. Does your desk have anything on it that might distract you from your work?
5. When studying, do you frequently skip the graphs or tables in your textbook?
6. Do you frequently make simple charts or diagrams to represent points in your reading?
7. When you find a word in your reading that you do not know, do you usually look it up in the dictionary?
8. Do you usually skim over a chapter before reading it in detail?
9. Do you usually glance through a chapter, looking at the paragraph headings, before reading it in detail?
10. Do you usually read the summary at the end of a chapter before reading the chapter?
11. Do you keep your notes for one subject all together?
12. Do you usually take your lecture notes in outline form?
13. Do you usually take your notes on reading in outline form?
14. Do you usually try to summarize your readings in a sentence or a short paragraph?
15. After you have read a chapter and taken notes on it, do you usually write a summary of the chapter as a whole?
16. Do you sit up studying late the night before an examination?
17. In preparing for an examination, do you try to memorize the text?
18. When you memorize something, do you usually do it all at one time?
19. Do you at times try to analyze your work to see just where you may be weak?
20. Do you often write an answer to a question and then realize that it seems to be the answer to some other question on the examination?
21. Do you consciously try to use facts you learn in one course to help you in your work in some other course?
22. Do you usually take notes in class just as rapidly as you can write?

Some years ago Luella Cole Pressey gave questions like these to 50 good students and 50 poor ones at Ohio State University. Good students more often than poor ones answered them as follows: (1) no, (2) yes, (3) yes, (4) no, (5) no, (6) yes, (7) yes, (8) yes, (9) yes, (10) yes, (11) yes, (12) yes, (13) yes, (14) yes, (15) yes, (16) no, (17) no, (18) no, (19) yes, (20) no, (21) yes, (22) no.

around for a minute. Pace the floor. Read out loud. Activity gets the adrenaline up. Another way of fighting sleepiness is to identify those times when you are likely to feel sleepy—for most people that is after meals—and schedule for those times the things you find easiest to concentrate on.

Different from but related to sleepiness is the feeling of being tired. After a period of reading or study you may feel mentally fatigued. Mental fatigue is not the kind of fatigue you feel after doing heavy physical work. For college students it is often the result of boredom and diminished motivation for study. Take this into account in making or revising your schedule. Study for shorter periods of time those subjects that tend to make you tired or fatigued. Schedule the longer stretches of studying for those subjects that absorb your attention.

The whole point is to maintain your schedule of study. Anything that keeps you alert is what you need. You may need to use a little ingenuity to discover what works for you.

STRENGTHENING BASIC SKILLS

How do your basic skills measure up? Are they up to the kind of studying you have to do? Some years ago, Luella Coles Pressey gave some questions like those listed on page 38 to 50 good students and 50 marginal students at Ohio State University. These questions appear to differentiate between good students and poor ones. Answer the questions yourself and compare the pattern of your answers with those given by good students.

Identifying Your Weaknesses

If you have answered the questions honestly, you will be able to pick out those aspects of your study skills that need improvement. Reading, for example, is a skill that most students take for granted. Many problems with reading you can identify yourself. Have you considered your reading speed? Nearly everyone *can* read faster than they actually *do* even without special speed-reading training. Do you adjust your reading speed to what you read? How much of what you read do you remember? Most students remember only about half of what they read right after they have read it. Can you decide what is worth trying to remember? Can you interpret charts, graphs, and tables? Do you understand the captions for charts, graphs, and tables? What do you do when you first start to read an assignment? How many times do you read an assignment? Do you read a textbook in chemistry or political science the same way you read a novel?

How well do you grasp the meaning of what you have read? Some students can read and correctly interpret whole sentences in an assignment, but they somehow can't put the sentences together. The passage makes no sense to them.

Do you take notes? Not all students do. What kind of notes do you take? Are they adequate? Do you sometimes have the feeling that the instructor springs things on you on the exams that were not in the lectures or in the reading assignments?

Some college students do not know the precise meaning of important words, words that instructors assume all students know. How good is your vocabulary? Do you pay attention to new words you encounter? Do you use the dictionary regularly? Do you know the difference between the general and the technical words you encounter? Can you identify technical words? Are you sure about the meaning of common prefixes and suffixes?

Many students are paralyzed by simple arithmetic or elementary algebra. Are you able to deal with fractions and decimals, to carry out the ordinary operations of addition, subtraction, multiplication, and division accurately and rapidly? Sure, you may say, I just use my handheld calculator. But what about those cases when that option is not available? Can you translate a word problem into the necessary arithmetic? Do you know how to deal with positive, negative, and fractional exponents? Can you solve an equation?

Correcting Your Weaknesses

Even the best students can't answer all these questions in the right way. When they do think that they know the answers, they are often wrong. But it is still a good idea to evaluate yourself by thinking about questions like these. In the chapters that follow, we give you some specific suggestions for getting the most from the classroom experience, improving your reading skills, studying textbooks more efficiently, taking examinations, writing papers, and studying foreign languages, mathematics, and the sciences. These suggestions, if you put them to use, will pay off in more efficient study, better grades, and greater satisfaction from your college experience.

3

The Classroom Experience

By now you know that college is different from high school. The demands are tougher, and you have to work on your own more than you used to. The relative importance of classwork and homework is reversed. In high school, you probably spent 25 to 30 hours a week in class and no more than a third of that doing outside reading and other assignments. In college you can expect to spend 15 to 18 hours in class and lab and about twice that time outside of class. That is one of the reasons we emphasize the skills you will need outside the classroom. But learning in both high school and college starts in the classroom, so that is where we begin.

HOW TO GET THE MOST OUT OF LECTURE COURSES

One of the biggest factors that determines the atmosphere of a class is the size. Some small colleges and a few private universities that have a relatively small student-to-faculty ratio may be able to maintain most classes at no more than 30 students and keep a few below 10. But most schools let the nature of the subject set the class size. Freshman English, math, and foreign language courses are taught in small sections because such courses require recitation and discussion. On the other hand, a lot of courses in your first year will be so large that no discussion will be possible. These classes are planned as a series of lectures. The teacher, who might well be an internationally known expert in the field, will do nearly all the talking. It doesn't matter, therefore, how many students are in the class because the instructor can just as easily talk to 300 as to 100 students. Even relatively small institutions have some of these large classes.

Attending Discussion Sections

Often small discussion sections offset the one-way flow of large lecture courses. These meet once a week in small groups, and the purpose of them is to allow students to ask questions and to put the lectures and readings into their own words. Because such teaching is time-consuming, it is usually done by graduate students or by junior members of the faculty, some of whom may be relatively inexperienced at teaching. Moreover, little new information is likely to be introduced in such sections. The result is that students who are not particularly interested in the subject have little incentive to attend. To provide such incentive, section leaders may give frequent quizzes.

Nevertheless, students are tempted to cut discussion sections, especially if the instructor appears to be inept. Before you start cutting, make sure that attendance is not required in your particular course. Your absence will be easily noticed, and you may find yourself with a lower grade as a result. If quizzes are given, it is your responsibility to find out when they are scheduled and what material they will cover. Then, even when sections are not particularly well taught, it is possible to get a lot out of them if you make the effort to do so.

Our advice to all students is to attend classes, even discussion sections, regularly. Even if the lecturer goes over the same ground as the textbook, it will probably be worth your while to attend. Students who frequently cut classes usually end up having academic trouble. After you have had some experience in college and know your own strengths and limitations, you may be in a better position to make sensible decisions about cutting classes.

Understanding How the Course Is Organized

Large courses are usually well planned. The instructor doesn't just assign a textbook, start lecturing, and periodically announce a quiz or exam. Most instructors pass out an outline or syllabus at the beginning of the semester.

This will include a schedule of the lectures, the reading assignments, and examination schedules. Students who are used to having assignments given every week or every day sometimes don't grasp the importance of the syllabus, and they may lose it or ignore it. Hang onto your course syllabus and consult it regularly. That will save you a lot of grief. Think ahead and make sure your schedule is clear for the exam dates. If you have a real problem being in class for a particular exam, consult your instructor or the teaching assistant as soon as possible. Most instructors will allow you an alternative date if you have a good reason for requesting one.

If you happen to be sick at the time of an examination, it is your responsibility to notify the instructor or teaching assistant and request a makeup exam. Instructors differ in their policy on makeups. Some refuse to give makeup exams, but most don't like them and some even assign handicaps or penalties to students who need them. So unless it is absolutely necessary, don't miss exams.

Some instructors will tell students how the test will be constructed. For instance, half may be based on lectures and half based on the reading assignments. Other instructors won't tell you, and they may even be annoyed if you ask. The best rule is to be prepared for any eventuality.

Many examinations in big lecture courses are *objective* in nature. These are tests in which you write little or nothing, but rather choose among alternate answers, mark statements as true or false, match words and phrases, or fill in the blanks. *Subjective* exams are those in which you are expected to write essays. The instructor will usually tell you early in the course what kinds of exams you will have. This is very important information, for the nature of the exam will determine how you study, as we point out later.

Another thing you will want to know about the course is how the lectures are related to the reading assignments. This is sometimes difficult to tell, but the syllabus should help. Look through the textbook and compare the topics with those listed as lecture topics. Some instructors will not cover anything in the readings, while others will follow the readings closely. Knowing ahead of time how the readings are related to the lectures will be a big help.

Improving Listening Skills

Listening to lectures in a large class may be boring. Being one of 300 people often makes you feel like you are part of a faceless herd that is being talked down to by some remote, impersonal figure. Because there is nothing to do but listen, some people slump in their seats, take no notes, daydream, or, worse, drift off to sleep. This last is the hardest thing to fight, but you can do it if you adopt the right attitude.

To be a good listener, you must participate in an active way. If you sit up straight, tell yourself that you are going to concentrate, and take notes, you will lessen your chance of falling asleep. Even if the lecture is a bore, keep your mind on what the lecturer is saying, not on his or her mannerisms or voice, the pictures on the wall, or the view out the window. You can learn something even from the worst lecturer. Taking good notes (to flesh out the preliminary notes you may have taken while reading the material covered) and keeping your mind on what is being said will pay you back at exam time. Many students don't even recognize what some of the exam questions are about, but if you don't go to sleep or daydream, you won't suffer from that handicap.

Taking Good Lecture Notes

Being a good listener and taking good notes go hand in hand. Some students can get by without taking notes, but they are a small minority, and you may not be one of them. A lot of students don't know how to take notes the right way even though they had some practice in high school. Some students scribble away frantically because they don't know how to pick out what is important. Others write down an isolated word or phrase that doesn't jog their memory later on. Whenever possible, make preliminary notes by reading the material that accompanies the lecture first. Then listen for key words during the lecture that correspond to your preliminary notes. Taking good notes from lectures is an art that develops through practice. It means that you must have an alert mind in class and that you must spend some extra time after class editing and rewriting notes. Time spent developing note-taking skills is time well spent.

Surveying, Questioning, Listening   A successful politician from the back-woods once explained how he gave speeches: "I tell 'em what I'm gonna tell 'em, then I tell 'em, and then I tell 'em what I told 'em." Good speeches, books, chapters, and articles give you some idea ahead of time about what is to come. When you read something, you can survey by skimming the headings and reading the summaries, but when it comes to lectures, you can't survey unless the lecturer does it for you. One of the best teachers we ever knew came into his lecture hall and put an outline of what he was going to say on the board. But don't count on that happening.

Try to pick up clues from what the lecturer says at the outset. When he or she says, "We're going to talk about the economic collapse of Germany after the Thirty Years' War," write that down. This gives you something to hang onto no matter how far the lecturer wanders from the topic.

Develop the habit of questioning the lecturer to yourself as the class proceeds. Use the few moments before class to think of questions that might arise about the topic of the day. Think like a reporter. Who? What? When? Where? Why? If all else fails, ask yourself, "What do I already know about this topic?" If you have a set of questions at hand, then you will be in the right frame of mind to take part in what is going on, even if that means only listening in an intelligent way. Keep asking questions of yourself during the lecture, even if it's only something like, "What is he talking about?" That will help you to be an active listener in what is going on although you are one of 300 faces in an amphitheater. Keep mentally active. That is the primary rule. Even a dull lecture can become interesting if you keep working at understanding what is being said. If we have one message above all others in this book, it is that effective learning demands active participation.

Getting the Organization   If you are going to understand what you hear, you will have to organize it in some way. Lecturers have little tricks to tell you about what is in their minds. A change in their tone of voice is one signal that they may be starting a new topic. They may be more explicit by using such throwaway phrases as, "And now let's turn to . . ." You now know to start a new heading in your lecture notes. Some lecturers talk so fast or are so deficient in their own organization that all you can do is to write down everything that seems important. If that is the case, you have to organize your notes into something coherent after class.

There are a few clues to help you provide that organization:

1. Statements that coincide with your preliminary notes are likely to be important points.

2. Statements such as, "The main point is . . ." or "Remember this . . ." tell you directly what the important points are.

3. Anything that the instructor says repeatedly is probably important.

4. Probably even more important is something the instructor says in three different ways.

5. A change in pace may serve as a clue; when a lecturer slows down and says something very deliberately, it is important.

Lecturers each have their own style. They all have different ways of telling you what is important. Get to know the style of your lecturers. Compare your reactions to those of other students in your study group. Other students may have picked up on something you missed.

Identify the major points the lecturer makes. Listening carefully will tell you that the lecturer organizes what he or she has to say into the equivalent of paragraphs and sections. Your job is to extract the essential information from those paragraphs. When you rewrite or edit or comment on your notes, do so in your own words. That way you will make sure that you understand what you have written down. Watch for technical definitions or other kinds of statements that are meant to be recorded word for word.

If you have trouble organizing your notes, remember that any notes are better than no notes at all. If the subject is new to you or if the instructor gives you so much information that you are overwhelmed, just try to get as much down as you can and to understand it. Sometimes it can only be organized when you put it together with what you pick up in your reading assignments.

The quantity of notes you take will depend on you and, of course, on the instructor. Practice note-taking. It is a skill that doesn't come automatically. But whatever you do, don't give up on note-taking altogether. Only a tiny minority of students can get by without notes. The chances are you are not one of them.

Reviewing and Revising

No matter how good they are, your lecture notes will be incomplete, imperfect, and not too well organized compared to your textbook. Revision helps. It also provides you with the chance to review and recite what you have learned. Review and recitation are the only tools you have to fight forgetting.

Your first review should be right after the lecture or as close to that as you can manage. That way you can fill in information you may not have written down while it is still fresh in your mind. The worst thing you can do is to let the notes go to the point at which you cannot even decipher them when you get around to trying to review them.

Don't rewrite notes mindlessly. Having them neatly copied may make them easier to read in the future, but copying will be an empty exercise if you don't engage your mind in what you are doing. This is probably a good place to comment on canned notes. At some large institutions you can buy published notes. These are okay as an auxiliary aid to studying, but don't let them substitute for your own notes, or, worse, substitute for going to class. Part of the learning process is in the writing of the notes with your own hand. Published notes are going to be, at best, a semester out of date, and they may even be for the wrong instructor. And, no matter how good they are, they aren't your notes you took yourself with all the thought and associations that went into taking them.

Keeping Lecture Notes

How should you keep your lecture notes? If you use a large, loose-leaf notebook, you should have dividers for each subject. You may prefer having a separate spiral notebook for each course. The trouble with that is that you may take the wrong notebook to class. Nothing is more inconvenient for study than a hodgepodge notebook in which several courses are jumbled together.

You will find that the standard-sized notebook is best for convenience of transportation and storage. Reserve the left-hand pages for notes from your reading and the right-hand pages for lecture notes that correspond to the reading notes. There should be ample room for marginal comments and copying. It cuts down on the amount of page turning you must do.

For lectures, date your notes; for textbook notes, indicate the chapters and pages. Do so for every page, so that you can tell at a glance where you are in reviewing your notes. If, for some reason, you are caught without a notebook or with the wrong notebook, transcribe your notes at the first possible chance.

The Five Rs of Taking Notes

Professor Walter Pauk of the Study Center at Cornell University once described five essential aspects of taking notes that he referred to as the five Rs. They are important enough to mention here:

    1. Recording. Get down all of the main ideas and facts.

    2. Reducing. To reduce is to summarize. Pick out the key terms and concepts. You can make from your notes what some students call "cram sheets."

Illustration of Reduced Notes

Original notes	Reduced notes

History 121   February 2, 200–

The Normans (cont'd)
I. Gov't of Henry II 1154–1189
  A. Chancery
    1. Documents became uniform.
    2. All executive orders dependent on written orders from king—per breve regis.
  B. Exchequer
    1. Administrative agents of the king: Sheriff, Viscount.
    2. Revenues were collected at Easter and Michaelmas.
      a. At Easter, Sheriff would pay one-half and be given a notched-stick talley as a receipt for what he had paid. He kept one-half, the exchequer the other.
      b. Revenues computed on principle of abacus.
    3. Every item of income was recorded year by year on pipe rolls (rolled skins of parchment). These are extant from second year of Henry II's reign.
  C. Judicial
    1. Tried to develop a system of courts and judges that would not require his personal intervention.
    2. Itinerant judges on circuit.
      a. Extended over all England.
      b. Broke down local privileges.
      c. Led to Common Law.
    3. Early court was an assembly of the king's barons; after Henry II the court became a body of professional judges.
II. Breakup of Anglo-Norman Empire . . .

The Normans (cont'd)
Gov't of Henry II 1154–1189
I. Organization
  A. Chancery
  B. Exchequer
  C. Judicial
II. Administrative reform
  A. Uniform documents
  B. Per breve regis for executive orders
  C. Sheriff, Viscount as administrative agents
  D. Revenues collected at Easter and Michaelmas
  E. Pipe rolls recorded yearly income
  F. System of courts
    1. Extended all over England
    2. Broke down local privileges
    3. Body of professional judges
    4. Led to Common Law

These are lists, usually in outline form, that give you the bare bones of the course. You can use them as cues for reciting the details of what you have learned. On each page of notes you take, allow room to write down such cues. An example of some notes and their reduction is illustrated above.

3. Reciting. The advice in item 2 suggests an important principle. Recite to yourself. Don't assume you know something just because you've read and understood it. You have to be able to tell someone else—your instructor—about what you have learned. So recite. In your own words.

4. Reflecting. Ideas from your course are meant to be thought about. Even though you may know that, you may not practice it. It's easy to fall into just giving back the information you have learned. Don't do that. In addition, if you reflect about what you are learning, you won't be surprised when ideas turn up on exams in an unexpected form.

5. Reviewing. The most important part of the art of studying is knowing when, how, and what to review. But however you do it, reviewing is essential. Even the accomplished performer—the pianist or the actor—knows that a review, no matter how well he or she may know the material, is essential to a professional performance.

By Way of Caution

Good students sometimes find eccentric ways of studying. If you are such a student, you may ignore nearly everything we've said. You may take notes on the backs of old envelopes if you want to. If you are really good at studying, you can get by with just about anything. But before you try, you had better be sure you are a virtuoso student. Even if you are, there are two pieces of advice you can't ignore. The first is to be active. Don't just listen passively. Argue with the instructor mentally. Be as aggressive as you can without actually challenging the instructor out loud. That is one of the easiest ways to make sure that you are active. The second, but even more important, piece of advice is to review. Few of us are gifted with the kind of memory that allows us to reproduce something new and difficult after only one exposure.

Contributing to the Discussion

Discussion classes are only as good as their contributors make them. Don't sit back and expect to be entertained. Not only will you not be doing your part, but also your instructor will probably notice. You may tell yourself, "But I can never think of anything to say." If that's the case, ask questions. It's hard to ask a dumb question. Don't be afraid to ask for information. That's what you're there for—to learn. When the instructor asks questions of the class, volunteer, even though you are not sure of the answer. Volunteering to answer questions is a good, active form of studying. Even if you are wrong, the instructor will sense that you are interested in what is going on and put you on the right track.

Exchanging Ideas with Classmates

Sometimes small recitation and discussion sections degenerate into discussions between the instructor and one or two students. A good discussion section is run like a seminar in which all students are expected to participate. What is more, students are expected to talk to one another, not just to the instructor. If you are lucky enough to be in a discussion section in which the students really do talk to one another, you will have experienced one of the best and most satisfying forms of education. In a really good discussion, the instructor needs to intervene only to get people back on track or to supply some missing information. But such a good discussion depends primarily on you, not the instructor.

HOW TO GET THE MOST OUT OF INDEPENDENT STUDY

Almost every college or university offers opportunities for independent study. Usually, such courses are taken for a variable amount of credit depending upon an agreement between the student and the faculty member. Sometimes these involve the student taking part in a research project sponsored by the faculty member. Whether you do original research, write an essay, or merely report to the faculty member on what you have read, independent study can be one of the best experiences of your college life. But as the phrase suggests, "independent study" requires some discipline.

Planning Your Work

If you are working on an independent project, it is tempting to put it off while you get your assigned chores out of the way. Don't fall into this trap. If you do, you will end up with an unfinished project and an incomplete for the course or, what is worse, a hastily done project and a poor grade. Students and faculty alike know that grades for independent study are inflated, and getting a C in independent study is like getting an F in a class. You will also have made a poor impression on the instructor from whom you may have to ask for a letter of recommendation.

So if you have an independent study course, get started immediately. Decide what you need to do and build time into your schedule so that you can do some work each week. If you plan to work in the library, set aside the necessary library hours each week. If you are working in a lab, make sure that you arrange for regular hours to use the lab. If your project requires that you do interviews or make observations in the field, schedule these so that you have all your data in time to prepare a final report.

As with any other course, make provisions to keep your notes or whatever else you need in an organized way. Nothing makes a worse impression on a professor than to have some student who is working on a research project come into his or her office with a handful of odds and ends of paper with penciled notes and data scrawled every which way on them.

Conferences with Your Faculty Adviser

Make sure you meet regularly, at least once a week, with your faculty adviser. Don't depend on your adviser to make the schedule. You do it. Faculty members have heavy demands on their time, and they are apt to forget about you or be hard to track down unless you have a regularly scheduled appointment. When a faculty member agrees to sponsor you in independent study, there is an implied commitment to spend time with you no matter how busy he or she is. Be prepared for each meeting; don't waste your adviser's time—or yours for that matter. Sometimes in independent study you will be part of a research team, and you will meet regularly as a group.

Preparing Your Paper or Final Report

The worst mistake students make in preparing a paper or final report is not allowing enough time to complete it. If it is a typical term paper, follow the procedures described in Chapter 7. If it is not a typical paper, make sure you know the form the final report will take when you begin to gather the material. Any independent project that you have worked on for an entire semester is worth the effort of a presentation that will do you justice. Don't let a hasty or sloppy presentation disguise all the good work you have done.

Sometimes when you prepare a final report in one of the sciences, the instructor will want you to follow the typical form of a scientific paper. If so, learn that format and gear your work to fit it.

Some Tips about Independent Study

Independent study can be one of the highlights of your college education, but don't overdo it. Law school admissions officers, graduate schools, and potential employers may look upon a student who spends half of his or her junior and senior years doing independent study with suspicion. That's because of the grade inflation that goes along with independent study. If you have done a great deal of independent study, be sure that you have copies of whatever you've produced. You may want to submit these with your graduate school application or give them to a prospective employer. But if you have put a lot of time in on independent study with little to show for it, those who look at your record will entertain the suspicion that you were really looking for easy As or a way to boost your grade point average without doing too much work.

If you do a really good job on an independent study project in, say, your sophomore or junior year, keep in touch with your adviser. He or she will know you well and will be able to write a good letter of recommendation for you.

A FINAL WORD

This chapter is one of the shortest in the book, and for good reason. We've already told you that in your college years you will spend about twice as much time outside of class as you will in class. In high school, you were taught mainly in class. In college, you teach yourself. It's not that going to class is not important–for most students it is an absolute must–but it has a different flavor in college. The chances are your high school teachers monitored your work carefully. That was part of their job. In most colleges, the role of the teacher is different. Your professor knows more than you do, and it is his or her job to transfer that information into your head or lead you to discover it for yourself, or better yet, to show you how to discover knowledge completely on your own. Learning is vastly easier if you go to class. If you take advantage of your new freedom to cut class, to sleep, or generally to goof off, you're in trouble. Once again, we remind you that if you find going to class such an awful chore that you can't get out of bed in the morning, you ought to think about whether or not you are ready for college. You can come back if you drop out, but it is much harder if you rack up a semester of Fs.

The Art of Reading

But thanks to my friends for their care in my breeding,
Who taught me betimes to love working and reading.

Isaac Watts (1674–1784)

Isaac Watts is a bit stuffy for modern tastes (he also wrote "For Satan finds some mischief still for idle hands to do" and "How doth the little busy bee improve each shining hour?"). But he has a point. You are lucky if you have learned to read well and you like to read. Usually, these things go together. What is certain is that if you are a poor reader, you will regard reading with all the enthusiasm you have for taking out the garbage. In college you must do more reading than you have ever done before, and if you don't read well, you need to improve your skills. Even if you are a good reader, the chances are that you can even be better at it. When you are better at it, you will like it more. This chapter is meant to help you improve your reading skills. Some parts of the chapter may help you decide whether you need special help in reading.

Here are some questions that are meant to help you decide if you are deficient in any of the most basic aspects of reading. Answer them carefully and honestly. If you can't answer a particular question, keep the question in mind. Then when you are next reading something–this book will do as well as anything–try to determine whether or not you have one or more bad habits in reading. Any question to which you answer yes indicates a fault.

1. Do you move your lips or vocalize when you read? Reading aloud is too inefficient for the modern world. When you move your lips, you are going through exactly the movements made in reading aloud. There are times, particularly if you are a fast reader, when you will have to slow down in order to understand something difficult. Then reading aloud may help. But most of the time it is terribly inefficient.

We could go on to say that moving lips is a bad habit that you ought to break. It is a bad habit all right, but it is a symptom rather than a cause of poor reading. Simply holding your lips still will not improve your reading, but if you learn to read better and faster, lip movement will disappear.

2. Do you read words one by one? Good readers know that some words are more important than others, and they do not give equal emphasis to each word. Reading words one by one is, like moving lips, a symptom rather than a cause of poor reading. People who read word by word have a hard time putting together the words to make sense out of them. They can understand each word as it comes, but they have no idea what the words are saying when they are put together in phrases and sentences. Many people who read this way are likely to write poorly and have a limited understanding of English grammar. If you think you read this way, you probably need some help from one of the study, learning, or reading skills centers at your college.

3. Do you often find words that you do not understand or that are unfamiliar to you in your assigned readings? If so, you need to work on your vocabulary. This is probably the easiest of reading problems to correct. We discuss some techniques for helping you to do this later in this chapter.

4. Do you backtrack and find it necessary to reread what you have just read? This is usually a symptom of inattention. Many times this happens because of fatigue. Sometimes, though, it happens because you have not learned the technique of putting ideas together as you read so that they make sense to you.

5. Do you read everything at the same rate and in the same way? Francis Bacon told us, "Some books are to be tasted, others to be swallowed, and some few to be chewed and digested." Some things need only be skimmed. Other things such as good stories can be read as rapidly as possible by a mixture of reading and skimming. Still others must be read very carefully; you must go through each sentence as if every word were a mine ready to explode. If you don't adjust your reading rate to the nature and difficulty of what you are reading, you are not a good reader. More about this in the next section, Reading for a Purpose.

6. Do you often complain that you don't understand what you read? Some things you won't understand. All of us at some time or other are going to have difficulty understanding what we read simply because we are ignorant of the technical details of the subject. If you don't know what a spreadsheet is, you can read an article on programming spreadsheets 50 times to no useful end.

You should be able to read *most* of the textbooks assigned to you. If you can't, there are several solutions. The obvious one is that you need some tutoring in the subject matter. But, then, you might just be a poor reader, something that you can correct by improving your basic language skills.

There are other faults, but these are the main diagnostic ones. If your reading is characterized by any of these things, you have room for improvement. And, as we mentioned earlier, everyone can improve his or her reading skills in some respect. There are a few people whose difficulties with reading are so fundamental and deep-seated that their problems must be described by a special word, "dyslexia." If you think you are dyslexic, you really need special help. But for most of you, just attending to a few details will improve your reading skills.

READING FOR A PURPOSE

Many students, when they sit down to study, just read. They don't think about the special purpose for which they are reading. The result is that they read everything—the comic pages, literature, history, chemistry, and political science—in the same way. But there are almost as many different ways to read as there are things to read. How you read should depend upon your purpose at the moment. That is mainly what the next few pages are about.

Skimming

One aim in reading is to find out what something is about. You may want to know what kinds of things are in a particular book, or if something you are interested in is mentioned, or if what the book discusses is something you already know. The way to find out is to skim.

There are several ways to skim. One is to look for signposts. That is easy to do in most textbooks and technical books because the headings do most of the work for you. You can leaf through a chapter and get a good idea of what it's about by just looking at the headings and subheadings. Another way to skim, particularly in books that don't have headings, is to look at the first sentence of each paragraph. Chances are that the first sentence contains the main idea of the paragraph. On the same principle, you may want to read the opening paragraph of each chapter or section. A third way to skim is to run your eyes over the page looking for key words. In many textbooks, key words are already highlighted in some way.

Skimming is a first step in studying. Because it is so important, we have more to say about it later in this chapter and in other chapters.

Getting the Main Idea

Sometimes we read just to get the main idea. Busy professional people do that, and it is a good thing to learn how to do. Often the whole purpose in reading is just to get the main idea and then use *your own* background of knowledge to pick up the details. Reading for the main idea is what you do in the first stage of study, as part of your survey; it is the last thing you do when you review.

How do you find the main idea? This depends upon what level of a book you are looking at. There are main ideas for entire chapters, sections, subsections, and paragraphs. Paragraphs are the smallest unit, and we start with them.

The usual definition of a paragraph, as a matter of fact, is that it is a section of prose that contains a single topic. Ideally, everything in the paragraph centers around that single topic (this doesn't always happen, you will understand, because even the best writers are not always alert). Incidentally, one of the ways you can help organize your own writing is to look for both main ideas and sloppy writing in what you read. We have more to say about that in Chapter 7. Learning to identify the main or topical idea in reading will help you with your own writing also.

In most writing courses you are told to begin a paragraph with a topic sentence, then explain it, illustrate it, support it with additional information, and finally wind it up with a summary statement or a transition to the next paragraph. That is good advice. However, it is not always practical or desirable to have the first sentence contain the topical information. Sometimes a transition sentence comes first.

A transition sentence shows the connection between one paragraph and the next, and, depending on the wishes and intentions of the author, it might be the first or the last sentence of the paragraph. (The last paragraph shows a transition sentence as the last sentence, and this paragraph shows a topical sentence as the first sentence. You can see how the transition sentence might very well have been the first sentence of this paragraph.)

Sometimes authors can't give you the main idea first. A common practice in textbooks is to illustrate a principle with an example or an analogy. This ties a new idea into something that the reader already knows. Keep in mind that the main idea is the principle and not the example or analogy.

Because locating the main idea is not always easy, we provide an example from a textbook on economics on page 58. In this example, it should be clear that the main idea is not always given as a complete sentence; sentences frequently contain more than one idea. The main idea is likely to be in the main clause of the sentence. You usually can boil that clause down to a few words. To see what we mean, pick up one of your textbooks and find some sentences with main ideas. Try throwing away the modifiers, keeping only the simple subject and the essential words in the predicate. The chances are you will have the main idea. (If you don't know what modifiers, simple subjects, and predicates are, you are in trouble. You need some help in English grammar.)

Sometimes, however, modifiers are important to the main idea of a topic sentence. For example, if you throw away the adjective in the sentence "Even tame lions bite," you will miss the point of the sentence. On the other hand, if you read, "The person who reads rapidly, scanning each line in the fewest number of glances and not stopping to daydream, is typically the person who learns a great deal in a short period of time," you can eliminate most of the words, translate them, and come up with, "The fast reader is usually a fast learner" as the main idea.

You may also find paragraphs in which the main idea is not expressed at all. That doesn't happen very often in textbooks, but it does in literature, and particularly in fiction. A writer may take a paragraph to describe a house. The purpose, however, is not to tell you about the house, but the description will tell you about the people in the house. From the description you may know, for example, that they are old, fussy, and aloof. You need to be alert to these kinds of things in reading imaginative literature.

Incidentally, almost nothing you read is complete in itself. Most writers don't tell you everything essential about a subject. A writer who did so would bore you beyond endurance. Every writer takes it for granted that you know certain things already—that you have had certain experiences—and that you can draw the necessary implications from what you read. If you don't understand something you read, it may be because you don't already know some-

Analyzing Paragraphs

Here are two paragraphs from C. R. McConnell and S. L. Brue, *Economics: Principles, Problems, and Policies,* 11th ed., The McGraw-Hill Companies, New York, 1990, p. 452. (This material was reproduced with permission of The McGraw-Hill Companies.) In the first of these paragraphs, we analyze the words and phrases to illustrate how to analyze paragraphs. The second paragraph is for your own practice. Underline the important words and phrases and then write your diagnosis of them in the margin.

Main Idea →

Explanation by Example →

Economists put forth the idea that specific consumer wants can be fulfilled with succeeding units of a commodity in the <u>law of diminishing marginal utility</u>. Let us dissect this law to see exactly what it means. A product has utility if it has the power to satisfy a want. <u>Utility is want-satisfying power</u>. Two characteristics of this concept must be emphasized: First, "<u>utility</u>" and "<u>usefulness</u>" are <u>by no means synonymous</u>. Paintings by Picasso may be useless in the functional sense of the term yet be of tremendous utility to art connoisseurs. Second, and implied in the first point, <u>utility</u> is a <u>subjective</u> notion. The utility of a specific product will vary widely from person to person. A bottle of muscatel wine may yield substantial utility to the Skid Row alcoholic, but zero or negative utility to the local temperance union president. . . .

← *Important Detail*

← *Important Detail*

← *Explanation by Example*

By marginal utility we simply mean the extra utility, or satisfaction, which a consumer gets from one additional unit of a specific product. In any relatively short time wherein the consumer's tastes can be assumed not to change, the marginal utility derived from successive units of a given product will decline. Why? Because a consumer will eventually become saturated, or "filled up," with that particular product. The fact that marginal utility will decline as the consumer acquires additional units of a specific product is known as the law of diminishing marginal utility.

---

thing needed to make sense out of the material or because you did not draw the correct implications from what was written. Consider the difference between a child reading *Alice in Wonderland* and an adult. The child likely will see only the interesting characters and the fantasy of it all. The adult will likely be wondering about the mental state of the author.

Practice finding the main ideas of paragraphs. If you do, you may become so skillful that you won't have to think about it. Not only will you have mastered one of the most important aspects of efficient reading, but you probably will have improved your own ability to write.

If you master the art of finding the main ideas from paragraphs, then finding the main ideas from sections and chapters will follow naturally. You will find yourself looking for the main ideas in everything you read. A textbook on psychology may contain a 20-page chapter on habits. That tells you what the chapter is about, but it does not tell you the main ideas in the chapter. To get them, you have to extract the essential information from each paragraph. So to find main ideas, concentrate on paragraphs.

Extracting Important Details

Frequently, students think that an instructor maliciously looks for unimportant or trivial details to use on examination questions. Most likely the reason for this thought is not the mean spirit of the instructor, but rather the student's inability to spot *important details* in the reading. Getting the main idea and remembering important details usually go hand in hand. If you have really grasped the main idea, then you can use it as a kind of tree on which you can hang the details. For example, if your history book tells you that, "The Congress of Vienna was a triumph of reaction," then you will be able to remember all sorts of important details—the restoration of the balance of power, the elimination of republican governments everywhere, and the attempt to reestablish old values and systems.

What is an important detail? It is often nothing more than an illustration of a general principle. This happens regularly in science texts. For example, a biology book may tell you that the sparrows in urban centers in England in the nineteenth century were darker and grayer than sparrows in the country. The text then goes on to tell you that this is an example of protective coloration and that it illustrates natural selection in action. City birds lived in an environment of sooty, coal-dust-stained stone rather than in the woods. The sparrows that were not easily seen by predators (alley cats, for example) survived to breed. The result was that urban sparrows became darker than their rural relatives. The important idea is that protective coloration results from natural selection. The sparrows just provide an example. If you are really onto the technique, you can probably come up with some examples of your own.

What is important is a matter of judgment, and people don't always agree in their judgments. But most of the time, particularly in textbooks, which are organized to present information in an orderly way, it is easy to pick out the main idea and *important* details. If you get in the habit of reading in such a way as to identify them without thinking about it, you will be a superior reader.

Reading for Pleasure

The more you read because you like to read, the better reader you will become. Some people read little more than *TV Guide,* the sports section of the newspaper, and supermarket tabloids, if that much. We don't mean to knock interest in any of these, but one of the things a college education should do for you is to expand the list of things you like to read. Also be aware that you can read for pleasure in all the same ways you read in order to learn. Some things you will want to read very slowly, even out loud or saying the words to yourself as you read. Other things you will want to skim. Some things you won't want to remember after you have finished reading them; others, you will. Some things you will want to read just for the way in which they are written, others because they tell you something you want to know. Our point here is that if you learn to like to read all kinds of things, your college education will have more than paid for itself.

Evaluating What You Read

Another thing that will guide your reading from time to time is *evaluation.* We hope that you will read controversial things, new stories, and other things that can't always be taken at face value. We even hope that you will read things that will offend your beliefs and values. The important thing is to evaluate—to determine why you agree or disagree with what you read. Even textbooks are sometimes not going to agree with your beliefs and preconceptions. When you disagree with something, use it as an opportunity to examine your own beliefs and determine whether or not you want to keep them. Sometimes you will say a resounding yes, and at other times you may want to change what you think in certain ways.

If you concentrate on evaluation as you read, it will keep you alert and you will absorb knowledge more selectively. You will become more skillful at dissecting arguments. We warn you, though, you won't be satisfied with accepting everything you read at face value.

Expanding What You Read

One of the really important purposes in reading is to expand or amplify what you read so that you can apply it to things perhaps not even imagined by the author. Sometimes you can apply what you read to your own problems. When you read this book, for example, certain things will apply to the way you do things, and others won't. Are you alert enough to expand upon things that apply and in so doing make this book more relevant to your own problems? Once again, this is part of making reading an active and not a passive process.

USING YOUR EYES

It may help you to improve your reading if you know something about what goes on when you read. You use your eyes, of course, when you read, but you use them in a special and in some respects a rather strange way. In this section we tell you how your eyes work when you are reading and how knowing that may help you improve your reading. You need to know, however, that your eyes are only tools. It is your purpose, your attentiveness, your knowledge, and your attitude that really determine what you get out of reading. When these are improved, proper use of the eyes almost always follows automatically.

Eye Movements

When your eyes move across a line of print, they move in a series of quick movements broken by very brief pauses. The movements are called "saccades." They are so fast that you are not aware of them. Your brain manages to blank out whatever signals come from your eyes during these saccadic movements. You are aware only of what you see during the pauses.

You aren't even really aware of the pauses, so it is easy to believe that your eyes move smoothly across the page. But if you watch another person read, you can clearly see the quick, jerky movements. Try it. Get someone, such as your roommate, to sit beside you and read. Then use a hand mirror to watch his or her eyes, and you can clearly see the pauses.

What you can't do, because they are so quick, is to count the movements. The pauses, which are called "fixations," last only one-fourth to one-fifth of a second. The number of pauses per line varies, of course, with the length of the line of print, the nature of the material being read, and your own skill at reading. Good readers fix, on average, once every three words of print. The typical college reader, however, is going to average about one and one-half words per fixation. Surprisingly, there is very little difference in the speed of the saccade between good and poor readers. About 90 percent of the total reading time is spent on fixations anyway, so the speed of the saccadic movements makes little difference.

The most important difference between good and poor readers is in something else—*regressive movements*. All of us move our eyes backwards from time to time while reading. Poor readers do it more often than do good readers, but there is another difference. Good readers go back to the beginnings of phrases and sentences, and they can pick out important and difficult passages to reread (because that is what regressive movements amount to). Poor readers just move their eyes back because they don't understand what they have just read.

Another difference between skilled and unskilled readers is in the return movement. Return movements occur when you move your eyes from the end of one line to the beginning of the next line. Good readers make a single, clean movement, while poor readers often overshoot or undershoot, so they have to make corrections to find the beginning of the line.

Improving Eye Movements

Eye movements in reading are automatic. That means that there isn't much you can do directly and consciously to improve them. In fact, knowing about them may make you a little uncomfortable and self-conscious about reading for a while. While some reading clinics have devices that may help to correct poor eye movement, one can accomplish this by improving the mental habits in reading. If you improve the way in which you approach reading, your eye movements will almost automatically become more efficient. One of the things that will help, however, is to keep a record of your reading speed. We have more to say about that later.

There is an upper limit to reading speed. You can't push your fixation time down to much less than one-fifth of a second. You can't increase the speed of your saccadic movements, and, even the best readers, unless they are skimming, must make a fixation, on average, about once every three words. Thus even if you make no regressive movements and if your return movements are absolutely on target, you can't read faster than 900 words per minute. No matter what anyone tells you, reading faster than that is skimming. Some things, of course, can be skimmed, and it is useful to know how to skim well.

Most people have a lot of room for improvement in reading speed. A typical student reads easy textbook material at a rate of between 200 and 300 words a minute. That rate can be pushed quite a bit higher, and, as it increases, your eye movements will improve.

HOW TO IMPROVE YOUR READING SKILLS

There are a few things nearly everyone can do to improve reading skills. Some of these will come naturally as you learn better study habits, for often poor reading is the result of wandering attention or an inability to organize what you are reading into coherent knowledge. But there are some specific steps—aside from general improvement in study skills—that will improve your reading ability.

Building a Vocabulary

If you're going to make sense out of what you read, you're going to have to enlarge your vocabulary as the material you read becomes more difficult. In college you are going to learn about a lot of things that are new to you. It stands to reason that you will acquire many new words. Many of these will be technical terms from certain disciplines. For example, if you take economics, you will learn about "demand curves" and "marginal utility." In psychology you will encounter "libido" and "ganglion." In philosophy you will be lost unless you grasp the meaning of "epistemology," "positivism," and "natural law." Furthermore, philosophers will use words you already know, such as "materialism" and "idealism," in very different and specialized ways. Technical terms aside, you will be asked to read books that contain words like "heuristic," "peroration," and "reticular." Knowing the vocabulary is often more than half the battle in the effort to understand what you read.

One of the most obvious signs of a good student is a strong vocabulary. Good students not only recognize and correctly define more words than do poor students, but they also discriminate more carefully among the multiple meanings of words. They don't often have to go back and say, "Huh, what was that?" To read efficiently, and thus faster, you should be able to perceive the meanings of words at a glance. You shouldn't have to stop and think. Paradoxically, one of the ways to help build a good vocabulary is to stop and look a word up you don't know.

Paying Attention to New Words   Be on the lookout for new words. When you see a new word or encounter one that you have seen before but which you can't pin down, don't pass it by. Not only is that being lazy, but it's a sure path to poor academic performance. The meaning of a whole sentence may hang on the new, unfamiliar word. And this may be the sentence with the main idea.

Using a Dictionary   The most important tool that a college student can have—even more important than a personal computer—is a good dictionary. Use it. Once you have spotted a new word, an old word in a new context, or

What You Can Learn from a Dictionary

Here is a reproduction of the entry for "memory" in *Merriam-Webster's Collegiate Dictionary, 10th Edition.** The entry tells you how to pronounce the word and how to spell the plural; it also tells you what part of speech the entry is (n = noun). It gives the etymology of the word (ME = Middle English; MF = Middle French; L = Latin). It then gives a series of definitions, and finally under synonyms (syn) it gives a number of words with similar meanings. A careful reading and study of this one entry can teach you about the correct use of a half-dozen words.

mem•o•ry \'mem-rē, 'me-mə-\ *n, pl* **-ries** [ME *memorie,* fr. MF *memoire,* fr. L *memoria,* fr. *memor* mindful; akin to OE *gemimor* well-known, Gk *mermera* care, Skt *smarati* he remembers] (14c) **1 a:** the power or process of reproducing or recalling what has been learned and retained esp. through associative mechanisms **b:** the store of things learned and retained from an organism's activity or experience as evidenced by modification of structure or behavior or by recall and recognition **2 a:** commemorative remembrance ⟨erected a statue in ~ of the hero⟩ **b:** the fact or condition of being remembered ⟨days of recent ~⟩ **3 a:** a particular act of recall or recollection **b:** an image or impression of one that is remembered ⟨fond *memories* of her youth⟩ **c:** the time within which past events can be or are remembered ⟨within the ~ of living men⟩ **4 a:** a device or a component of a device in which information esp. for a computer can be inserted and stored and from which it may be extracted when wanted **b:** capacity for storing information ⟨four megabytes of ~⟩ **5:** a capacity for showing effects as the result of past treatment or for returning to a former condition—used esp. of a material (as metal or plastic)

syn MEMORY, REMEMBRANCE, RECOLLECTION, REMINISCENCE mean the capacity for or the act of remembering, or the thing remembered. MEMORY applies both to the power of remembering and to what is remembered ⟨gifted with a remarkable *memory*⟩ ⟨that incident was now just a distant *memory*⟩. REMEMBRANCE applies to the act of remembering or the fact of being remembered ⟨any *remembrance* of his deceased wife was painful⟩. RECOLLECTION adds an implication of consciously bringing back to mind often with some effort ⟨after a moment's *recollection* he produced the name⟩. REMINISCENCE suggests the recalling of usu. pleasant incidents, experiences, or feelings from a remote past ⟨recorded my grandmother's *reminiscences* of her Iowa girlhood⟩.

a word you think you know but are not sure about, the first thing to do is to look up the word in a dictionary. We repeat: *Your dictionary is the single most important study aid you own.* Make sure that the dictionary you buy is a good one. Spend a little more to get a well-edited, sturdy dictionary that is intended to be used at the college level. It will be used hard. If you have easy access to the Internet, there are some good dictionaries available online.

*By permission. From *Merriam-Webster's Collegiate® Dictionary, 10th Edition,* © 2002 by Merriam-Webster, Incorporated.

When you look up a word in a dictionary, find the meaning for the particular context in which the word appears. Many words have a general meaning, but they also have particular meanings in particular subjects. A good dictionary will give you those, though it may be way down in the entry. So when you look up some word, don't just settle on the first meaning that is listed; look through the whole entry. An example of the kinds of things a dictionary entry can tell you about a word is shown on page 64.

Every educated person should acquire the dictionary habit. Accomplished writers, who have a better command of English than most people, often have half a dozen dictionaries for different purposes. They are forever looking up new words and even words they have used all their lives simply to sharpen their understanding of the language.

Vocabulary Cards and Other Aids   If you have a poor vocabulary, you will have to work extra hard to do something about it. One good old-fashioned way is to use vocabulary cards. Three- by five-inch index cards are best for this purpose. Carry some around with you, and, when you come to a new word or a word about which you have some question, write it on a card. It would probably also be a good idea to write some hint about the context in which you found the word. Then, when you have access to a dictionary, look up the word and write its definition on the other side of the card.

When you have accumulated a batch of cards, take the cards out and look at the side with the new word. Try to recite the meaning of the word, and then turn to the other side to see whether or not you were correct. Some people keep tabs on themselves by putting a dot on a corner of the card each time they miss the definition. These vocabulary cards are particularly helpful when you are in a course that makes heavy use of technical terms. Some people use the technique for general self-improvement. They set goals for how many new words they are going to learn each week.

This technique could be modified for use on a computer, but cards are much more portable. To be useful, the cards must be available at all times; you never know when you will find an unfamiliar word. Many people believe that they can dispense with dictionaries because of the spell-check feature in word processing software. Spell check will not catch incorrect word choices such as *there, their,* and *they're,* or *for, fore,* and *four.* It is true that we use dictionaries less than we used to for spelling, but that is not the purpose of the cards. The cards are meant to get you to *know* the word, especially the definition. Spell check does not do that.

You may also buy some canned programs—either for computers, CDs, or tape recorders—for building vocabulary. These are useful, but they are not nearly as useful as cards you make yourself. First of all, with canned programs you are a passive observer or listener rather than an active participant. Second, you are the victim of what the authors of the program think you ought to learn, not what you choose for yourself. We feel that the best use of such programs is in your car tape deck when you are on long trips or stuck in traffic.

General versus Technical Terms   We've already referred to the distinction between general and technical words. Be sure to remember that distinction when you are building your vocabulary. For many technical words or technical uses of ordinary words, you should consult a specialized dictionary or a glossary. Many textbooks have glossaries of technical words. Use them. If you are going into a specialized field such as medicine or law, you may want to own a dictionary that is essentially a glossary for that field. These specialized dictionaries are expensive, but are often worth the money. If you have any doubt that you are using a technical term correctly, consult the appropriate dictionary.

Technical terms are more important than students realize. In some courses, more than half of the subject matter is in knowing what the terms mean. List these terms separately and study them. Make up your own glossaries.

Dissecting Words   You can improve your vocabulary by learning how words are constructed. English is a complicated language with many roots. Some words are Germanic, some Latin, some Greek, and still others French. We have also borrowed words from virtually every other language on Earth. In the kind of reading normally found in college, there is a heavy Latin influence. Words with a Latin influence are built from elements many of which are used over and over again in different combinations to produce new words. There are three basic kinds of elements: prefixes, suffixes, and roots. If you know the meaning of the root of a word and the meanings of any prefix or suffix attached to the word, then you have a good shot at guessing the meaning of the word itself.

The root is the main part of a word. The prefix and suffix are syllables added to the beginning and end. In the word "premeditation," for example, "pre-" is the prefix, "meditate" is the root, and "-ion" is the suffix. The prefix "pre-" means before, and the suffix "-ion" tells you that the word is a noun.

"Meditate" means to contemplate or think about. Thus premeditation is an act of contemplating something in advance. So if you read that someone was murdered with premeditation, you will know that the murderer thought about it beforehand; it was not an accident.

In a separate table (pages 68 and 69) we have listed some of the more common prefixes and suffixes. Guess at the meanings of these. We have provided space for you to write your definitions. Check the definitions in a dictionary and, if yours were off the mark, review the correct meanings.

There is also a short list of some common Latin roots and their meanings. Since most of you will not have taken Latin, it would be unfair to expect you to know the meanings of these roots, although you can make an informed guess at any English word that contains one of these roots. These Latin roots appear over and over again in a large number of English words.

If you have a good dictionary, the chances are that it will give you something of the origin of the word in question—its etymology. For example, one of the dictionaries commonly used by college students tells us that "domestic" is an adjective and that it derives from the Latin word "*domesticus,*" a word itself based on another Latin word, "*domus,*" meaning house. The word did not come directly from Latin into English, however. Instead, the dictionary tells us, it is directly derived from the French word "*domestique.*" There are two major routes by which Latin words entered English. The older route is through French. If you have studied English history, you know that the language of the ruling classes in England after the Norman Conquest in 1066 was French. When the nobility began speaking Anglo-Saxon, they incorporated many French words into what became modern English. The later route by which Latin words entered English was a direct one. That was partly because in the Middle Ages, books and other documents began to be written in English rather than in Latin or were translated from Latin to English. Either way, many of the Latin words remained or were pressed into service.

Some Greek words have found their way into English, mostly by way of Latin. While Greek-based words are encountered much less frequently than words of pure Latin origin, some of them are very important. "*Logos,*" which in Greek had a broad spectrum of meanings including word, speech, symbol, thought, and knowledge, is the basis for the English word "logic" and for the suffix "-ology" (as in psychology, sociology, etc.), as well as the root of words such as "prologue." Greek words can be found in a number of words coined by scientists, but not nearly as frequently as Latin roots.

Common Prefixes, Suffixes, and Latin Roots

The prefixes and suffixes listed below occur often in English words. Any good dictionary will list and define almost all of them. You can help improve your vocabulary by looking up their meanings and writing them in the space provided. Also listed are a few of the many Latin roots upon which English words are based. The English meaning is given for each. Try writing beside each root as many English words derived from it as you can.

Prefixes	Meaning
ab-, abs- a-	
ad-, a-, at-, ap-	
be-	
bi-	
co-, com-, con-	
de-	
dis-	
en-	
in-, il-, im-, ir-	
non-	
per-	
pre-	
pro-	
re-	
sub-	
un-	

Suffixes	Meaning
-able, -ible, -ble	
-al	
-ance	
-ent	
-est	
-ful	
-ing	
-ion	
-ity	
-ive	
-ize	
-less	
-ment	
-ous	

Common Prefixes, Suffixes, and Latin Roots (*Continued*)

Some Common Latin Roots	English Equivalent	English Words Containing Them
capio	take, seize	
duco	lead	
facio	do, make	
fero	bear, carry	
mitto	send	
muto	change, alter	
probo	test	
recipio	take back	
specto	look at	
tendo	stretch	
terreo	frighten	

Learning to Read Faster

We've already pointed out that there is an upper limit to how fast anyone can read. Most of us, however, seldom come close to that upper limit, so there is room for improvement. Also, sometimes we read when all we need to do is skim. Those of you who have taken one of these so-called speed-reading courses may know that you can skim a whole page in seconds. However, you can also skim in a more detailed way, so that you pick up almost as much information as you would in reading. In fact, good readers usually mix skimming and reading, and all good readers adjust their rate to the difficulty or unfamiliarity of the material.

Practice at Reading   "I get plenty of practice at reading," you might say. "I read several hundred pages each week." True enough. As a college student you do get a lot of practice. But practice doesn't necessarily lead to improvement. In order to improve your reading speed, you must have a way of measuring your reading speed. The first step toward improving your reading speed is to keep a record of how fast you read. You will find a chart on page 70 in which you may record your results.

Set aside a special time each day to train yourself to read faster. It can be at any time, as long as you are consistent. Don't let other activities interfere with this activity. Plan on spending a half-hour at your practice each day.

Chart for Increasing Reading Speed

Use this chart to keep track of your progress in your daily practice in reading faster. For instructions see text (to find reading rate, multiply the number of pages by the number of words per page and then divide by time).

Magazine or book	Pages	Time	Rate

Choose something that you like to read: a novel, a book of short stories, or a magazine such as *Time* or *Newsweek* would do well. Try to choose something that will not distract you with pictures and that does not ask you to look at tables, graphs, or formulas. Whatever you choose, keep the same kind of material for the duration of your self-training course. If you choose something like *Time,* which has multiple columns and an irregular format, keep on reading that kind of material. If you choose a book with only a single column per page, keep reading books with the same format.

Using a timer, record the time to the second that it takes to read three or four pages. Divide the total number of words you have read by the number of minutes. You don't need to count all the words. Count the words in ten lines and the total number of lines you have read. Then find the approximate number of words by multiplying the number of words in ten lines by the number of lines and then divide by ten. Record the results in the chart. You will also find it helpful to make a graph that shows the change in your reading rate. Put on the horizontal axis of the graph the number of the practice session—first, second, third, etc.—and on the vertical axis put the number of words per minute that you read. Make a mark on the graph for the reading rate at each practice session. That way you will not only be able to tell if you are improving but also if you are improving steadily. Make sure that you do not sacrifice comprehension for speed. You will need to check from time to time to see how much you remember of what you read. You can do this informally just by trying to summarize the material that you have read.

If you are typical, you should reach a *near* maximum rate of reading after a couple of weeks of daily practice sessions. You can tell from your graph when the rate of increase in reading speed levels off, that is, when you are not showing significant improvement. This will not be the best you can do, but it is a good start. Then it is time to begin practicing with more difficult material such as the textbooks you use. You will need to work on material in which there are unfamiliar words and in which the sentences are long and complicated.

If you are doing things correctly, you should be reading more slowly during the first few sessions with the difficult material. At the same time you should be conscious of reading your regular assignments more rapidly and efficiently. Reading efficiently means gearing your reading speed to the difficulty of the material. You will also need to practice moving back and forth between reading and skimming. The chances are that you can improve your reading skills all your life. The biggest improvements are going to come early, however, and just a few weeks of practice will be a big help, particularly if you are not a good reader to begin with.

If, when you start out to measure your reading speed, you find that you are a very slow reader—that is, you cannot read easy material at more that 150 words per minute—try to find some place for remedial work. Most colleges have such places, though they go by a variety of names. Consult your adviser, a teacher, or a friend to find out where you can go to get help in reading. If after a good try on your own, you cannot read easy material faster than 250 words per minute, the chances are you are doing something wrong. Again, look for help.

Practice Skimming   There are two ways to skim. One is to look for key words or phrases that represent the ideas that you are looking for. Suppose we wanted to research the topic from a few pages back about how Latin words came into English. We might look for a book or article on the general topic and then skim, looking for entries such as "Latin," "Norman French," "growth of the vernacular," and similar words or phrases. Very soon you would find the portions of the material that you would want to read more carefully.

Another kind of skimming is the kind you do when you pick up something new. You just let your eye wander down the page, getting a feel for what the book or article is about, how it is written, and what kind of vocabulary is used. It is a kind of scouting expedition that, among other things, can tell you how fast you are going to gear your reading rate.

More useful to most people is a mixture of reading and skimming that we might call "browsing." When you browse through a book, you let your eyes run down the page, catching a word or phrase here or there. When you find something interesting or important, you read it in detail. We ordinarily think of browsing as a kind of passive activity—the sort of thing we do when we are in the dentist's office—but it really isn't because it requires you to be alert to the kinds of things you might be interested in.

Browsing is a good technique for looking over secondary reading—the kind of material your instructor may put on reserve in the library. Make it a practice early in the semester to browse through some of or all the books on reserve. You'll get an idea of what they are about and how difficult they are. When you find something that interests you later in the course, you will have a good idea of where to go. And, of course, if you have a term paper to write, browsing at the beginning of the semester may prevent that panic about what you are going to write about.

Studying from Textbooks

Let's assume that you have read the first four chapters of this book and have tried to carry out the advice in them. You have made a workable schedule, found a good place to study, and assured yourself that your reading skills are up to college level. You understand the plan of the course you are taking, have set up a notebook in the right way, and have begun to take notes.

You have a copy of the textbook for the course, and it is on your desk along with all the other materials you need, including a notebook and writing implements. You are now ready to read the assignment in the textbook. How do you make the best use of the time you've allotted for this study period?

FIVE STEPS TO EFFECTIVE STUDY

Every student has a unique approach to studying textbooks. Two students, both outstanding, can go about studying the same material in very different ways. There are, nevertheless, some general principles for effective study of textbooks. People who are good at studying use these rules in one way or another, even people who don't realize they are doing so, just as the man in Moliere's play was surprised to discover that he had been talking prose all his life. Where they will differ is mainly in their individual styles and the degree to which they emphasize different aspects of the principles of good studying.

What are these principles? One way of phrasing them originated with the late Francis P. Robinson of Ohio State University, who spent a long career guiding students in their study habits. Robinson put it in a formula: Survey Q 3R, or simply SQ3R. It is a good slogan and one that is easy to remember. It is a way of summarizing the five specific steps in effective study. These steps are:

1. Survey

2. Question

3. Read

4. Recite

5. Review

Robinson's plan has been widely adopted. Although there have been suggestions to change it in minor ways, it is still, after all these years, a very good approach to studying from textbooks. It is something that all students, good and poor, can do, and if they do, their study habits will improve.

Survey

The first of the five steps is to survey. This is how you get the best possible overview of what you are going to be reading before you study it in detail. Surveying does for you when studying a textbook what reading a map does for you before you take a trip on unfamiliar roads. You know what you are going to run into before you start.

Surveying a Textbook   Surveying a textbook is done in steps from big ones to little ones. When you first pick up a book, look at the whole book. Start by reading the preface to get an idea of why the author wrote the book. Also by reading what the author has to say in the preface, you can find out what kind of textbook it is and for whom it is written. It may even tell you what background you need for reading the text.

Next, look at the table of contents. Find out what's in the book. You will want to do this several times as you get into the course. The more you read in the book, the more meaning the table of contents has.

Finally, leaf through the book. In a short period of time you can turn every page of a good-sized textbook, glancing at the headings, reading sentences here and there, and looking at the illustrations. The effort is worth it. You will have a feel for what is in the book, how difficult it is, and how it is organized. More and more textbooks these days have chapter summaries. Skim these too.

Surveying a Chapter   When you settle down to read a chapter, look through it first. When most authors write textbooks, they go to some pains to organize what they have to say under various headings. They do this mainly to let you know what to expect. In many textbooks it is hard to find a page without one or more headings.

Yet many students ignore the headings and try to read textbooks as they would read novels. When they do that, they ignore the most significant and useful clues to the content of the text. Use headings. Try to think as you read why the author used the heading. Many times it is the main idea of a section. This is part of the active, as opposed to passive, process of reading.

Pay attention to the *level of headings*. Most textbooks use two or three levels of headings much like in an outline. In some textbooks, the heading scheme may be more or less complicated with different levels of headings distinguished by type size or style.

We have gone into some detail about headings because you use them at nearly every stage of the study process. We also know that most students do not do enough surveying. They've acquired the habit of plunging right into the text without first making a map of what they are going to find, and the headings are the signposts.

Question

The Q in SQ3R stands for *question,* and it emphasizes the importance of asking questions while you are learning. Most things worth remembering are answers to some sort of questions. Moreover, people seem to remember better what they learn as an answer to a question rather than things they have merely tried to memorize. This is probably because asking oneself questions is a more active process than trying to memorize, and it also tends to focus attention on the answers as you read.

Your Questions   If you make use of the question technique in reading this book, you should already have a number of them about this section. Why is asking questions so helpful? What kind of questions should I ask myself? Should I write them down? These are some of the things you might have asked by now. Some questions have already been answered for you, and if you keep the others in mind, you will find that most of them will also be answered. But if you are clever about asking questions, you may come across something we didn't think about. You will have to answer those kinds of questions for yourself.

Our major point here is that you are the best source of questions because you are the one who knows what you are trying to learn, and you are aware of what you already know. How do you go about asking the right sort of questions? The most direct way is to use the headings. A simple question is "What is ____?" This will happen most often when you are reading something technical and when the heading takes the form of a technical phrase. For example, in a textbook on astronomy, you might find the phrase "retrograde motion." Your question is "What is retrograde motion?" If you can't get a clear definition from the section with that heading, you need to consult either other parts of the same book (an index or a glossary) or some other source.

Some people advocate writing down questions, but we don't. It is time-consuming, and eventually the art of asking questions will become so habitual that you won't even be aware of forming them. Remember, the main purpose of asking questions as you read a textbook is to direct you to the main idea in a section and to help you assimilate that idea into what you already know.

An example of the types of questions that might occur to you about a portion of text is shown on page 77.

The Author's Questions   Although you are the best source of questions, the author of the book you are reading may provide you with some. Use them. They are often the most neglected part of a textbook, particularly when they are stuck at the end of the chapter.

Author's questions have many uses. You can use them in your survey. You can use them while you read and again when you have finished reading as a way of testing yourself. If you test yourself before the instructor does, you will have a much easier time on examinations.

Workbooks accompany some textbooks, particularly in the social sciences and the natural sciences. If the workbook to a text you are studying has questions, use them to tell you what you don't know and to suggest questions to ask about the main text.

The Use of Questions

Here is an excerpt from a textbook (Janet L. Hopson and Norman K. Wessells, *Essentials of Biology*, The McGraw-Hill Companies, New York, 1990, p. 28. This material was reproduced with permission of The McGraw-Hill Companies.). The kind of questions you would want to ask about this excerpt are written in the margin.

Why is water slow to change temperature?

What does this property provide for living creatures?

What is cohesion?

Adhesion?

Tensile strength?

Capillarity?

Because of its high specific heat, water is slow to change temperature, and considerable amounts of heat must be added or removed to make the temperature change much. This property provides special insurance for living creatures, which often function best within a narrow temperature range. The seawater surrounding a kelp or a barnacle, as well as the water within the organisms, tends to heat or cool more slowly than the surrounding air or soil, and this provides a natural buffer against potentially damaging temperature fluctuations.

Water molecules also exhibit physical properties, such as strong cohesion, adhesion, tensile strength, and capillarity. **Cohesion** is the tendency of like molecules to cling to one another (such as water to water). **Adhesion** is the tendency of *unlike* molecules to cling together (such as water to the molecules of silicon dioxide on the walls of a drinking glass). **Tensile strength** is related to cohesion and is a measure of the resistance of molecules to being pulled apart. And **capillarity** is the tendency of molecules to move upward in a narrow space against the tug of gravity.

Here is another excerpt from the same source (p. 29). Try writing your own questions.

Let us see how these properties apply to some easily observed biological phenomena. You can observe the results of adhesion when you pour water into a flowerpot full of soil. The water sinks in and "wets" the soil, rather than remaining on top, because of water's inherent "stickiness," its tendency to adhere to the dissimilar molecules in the soil. Adhesion, cohesion, and capillarity also help explain why much of the water remains in the soil rather than running straight through. The molecules of water can resist the downward tug of gravity by first adhering to the surface of soil particles and then moving into tiny air spaces between them via capillarity. The water molecules enter the spaces and pull others along by means of cohesion, and thus remain in these tiny spaces rather than flowing out the bottom of the pot.

Read

The next step to effective study is reading. Any book, of course, is meant to be read. But reading is not the first, last, or necessarily even the most important part of studying a textbook. It provides the details. It fills out the framework you should already have if you have been surveying.

Keep your notebook handy when you read your textbook. Sort out what you deem to be the important points and write them on the left side of your notebook (the even-numbered pages). Use them during the corresponding lecture to flesh out the material that your instructor thinks is important.

Reading Actively   Many things you can read passively. A good detective story or a column in the sports section of the newspaper are written mainly for your entertainment. You don't need to worry about remembering things because either you will (to tell your friends about) or you won't. It isn't that important. The kind of reading you will have to do in a literature course is likely to be a different matter. You must read in such a way that there is a kind of dialogue between you and the author.

Most textbooks need to be explored. You can't just walk through them. You have to be alert to them every step of the way. Questioning while you read is one way to avoid reading passively. You must keep asking yourself, "Am I following what I am reading? Can I remember what I have just read?" Stop every so often and try yourself out. If you do this, you will no longer voice the familiar complaint: "My head is just like a sieve; I forget what I read the minute I am through."

Reading important novels, plays, poetry, and stories requires more than passive reading, but the specific recommendations we give here do not necessarily apply to them. They require a different set of skills. Toward the end of this chapter we have a few words to say about reading history and literature. What we have said so far mainly applies to books that you read to get the information that is in them.

Reading for Important Details   Thus far we have said that when you read a textbook, you read for the main ideas. But you also have to pick up the details—examples of a principle, historical anecdotes, things that you can hang on the main ideas.

Noting Important Terms   Authors have ways of telling you what is important—they use italic or boldface type for key words and phrases. These are signs to stop and pay attention.

If a technical term is italicized or set in bold type, repeat it to yourself and make sure you know what it means. Also, though you may think it is a small point, make sure you know how to spell technical terms. Instructors sometimes get impatient with students who can't seem to learn to spell important words.

Let's face it, authors do not always emphasize important words or phrases by italic or boldface type, in which case you will have to look after that for yourself.

Reading Graphs, Tables, and Illustrations   When you read, read everything. One of the worst things you can do is skip tables, graphs, and diagrams. Give them more than a casual glance. Authors put things in diagrams and graphs for a reason. Even a simple photograph or drawing can tell you what a whole section is about. It is true that some textbooks have pictures just because they are pretty. Can a picture of Henry IV in the snow outside of Canossa help you remember things about the conflict between the Holy Roman Emperors and the Pope? Maybe. (We have more to say on the topic of tables and graphs in Chapter 9.)

Recite

Long before books were common, recitation was the heart of learning. In parts of the world today where the tradition of using books is not firmly established, recitation is still the primary means of learning. Have you seen a documentary about some school in a remote part of the world in which all the children recite in unison? Such rote recitation is less valuable than the kind we are concerned about here because it favors memorization over understanding and questioning. Rote recitation does have its uses, however. Getting the multiplication tables into your head so that you can do fast calculations when you don't have your handy pocket calculator requires a lot of plain rote recitation. To a lesser extent rote recitation can also be applied to the study of foreign languages and similar things. But our main emphasis here is on reciting for comprehension and recall.

Reciting as a Means of Recall   You may believe that if you read your textbook, you understand it and can recall what you have read. But if you recite to yourself, you may make the unpleasant discovery that you don't really remember.

The best way to find out if you really understand and can remember what you have read is to recite to yourself just after you have finished reading. Try to say in your own words what the author said. Recitation is an effective study method not only because it forces you to read actively but also because it immediately reveals to you your ignorance. If you recite, you can correct yourself on the spot.

Reciting is a means of recalling. Stop as often as you need to and try to recall what you have just read. You might, right now, stop and ask yourself what you have learned in this chapter. What are the main ideas? What are the general principles and the details that support them? Check your recall against the book.

The general rule is as follows: As you read, stop at intervals to recite the substance, in your own words, of each major section in a chapter. When you do your first reading of the material, the amount of time you spend in reciting will probably be less than that spent actually reading. But when you review for an examination, most of your time should be spent reciting rather than reading.

Recitation both at the original reading and at the review is necessary. Older research on the value of recitation for remembering showed that the earlier you recite, the less you forget later on. The first recitation helps to keep the forgetting process from getting started. Because some forgetting is almost inevitable no matter what you do, you need that review just before the examination to correct for the fact that you will have forgotten some things despite your earlier review.

More recent research tells us why early review is important. Remembering the kind of thing you find in a typical textbook is not merely remembering how to string words together, as you might do in trying to remember a poem in a language you don't know. When you read something you understand, you form a structure in your own way of thinking. Just reading is a lazy process; the structure you form from just reading may be so simple and bare of detail that it will never do for an examination. In one investigation in which college students were asked to write down what they had just read, some students read so superficially that all they could say was, "This passage was about how evolution makes different species of animals." All the details in the passage about the classification of animals, about the relationship between genetics and evolution, and about natural selection were ignored.

How Much Recitation?   The amount of time you should devote to recitation depends on the material that you are studying. If it is something rich in detail and full of confusing relationships or unrelated facts, you need to spend a lot of time reciting. That is because it is hard to form a rich structure for such material in your head. In some cases you may want to spend as much as 90 percent of your time in recitation. If, for example, you have to learn a number of rules, items, names, laws, or formulas, then recitation should be your principal mode of study.

If, on the other hand, the material is well organized or in the form of a story or historical narrative, less recitation is required. You may only need to pause here and there to make sure you know names and dates. It is hard to recommend a precise figure, but perhaps as little as 20 percent of your total study time should be spent in recitation. For courses such as economics, political science, and the like, 50 percent of your time may be spent in recitation. But remember, these are ballpark figures. How much time you actually spend in recitation will depend upon how active your normal reading is (if you read attentively all the time, you needn't spend so much time reciting), the particular course, and a lot of other circumstances.

This you can be sure of: The time spent in recitation pays off. One famous study showed that students who spent up to 80 percent of their time reciting did better than those who spent the same amount of time reading without reciting. Also, the time you spend reciting actually saves time. The amount you remember when you recite is so much greater that you don't need to spend nearly so much time in rereading and review.

When do you stop to recite? To wait until the end of a chapter is to wait too long. On the other hand, stopping to recite every paragraph—with some exceptions—is too much. It breaks up the material; you can't form sensible structures because you haven't completed enough reading to do it with. Your best guides are the headings. Stop each time you get to a new heading and recite what you have read in the section you have just finished.

Besides giving you a chance to put things in your own words, recitation keeps you attentive. When you just read, it is easy to do so with only half a mind—to read the words without really taking them in. When you know you have to recite something, you can't daydream.

Recitation also helps you correct mistakes. It shows you where you have missed something or where you have misunderstood it. If you make notes of these mistakes when you recite, you'll know exactly what points you're going to have the most trouble with.

Review

The fifth and final part of SQ3R is review. We don't need to make a big thing out of this because most students review anyway before examinations (assuming they have studied before exam time). We can, however, make suggestions about how to review and when it should be done.

Surveying the Material   Reread enough to make sure that you haven't omitted anything and to refresh your memory. Recite both before and after you read. The recitation before reading a section will tell you how carefully you need to read again. Reciting after your reading will tell you what you have learned. If you have taken notes on what you have read, use these to guide your reviews and as a prompt for the recitation before your review.

When to Review   If you have done a good job at surveying, questioning, reading, and reciting, you won't have trouble knowing what to do when you review and how often to review. Most students wait until just before an exam to do their reviewing. This is a good time for review, but really careful students review before that time as well.

The first time to review is immediately after you have studied something. For example, after you have read a chapter, reciting after each of its sections, you should immediately go back and review it. This means trying to recite the important points of the whole chapter and rereading as necessary to check yourself. This first review may be fairly brief, but it is important.

If you are really well organized, you will plan for one or two reviews between the first review and the final review before an examination. These intervening reviews are the ones most often skipped by students, but they make the final review easier.

The final review should consist of as much unprompted recitation as possible. Use the book to check the accuracy of your recitation, but try to recite without reading first. Go over all the material you think you will be responsible for. Plan your time so that you can review *all* the material. You don't want to run out of time when you are halfway through. It goes without saying that trying to cram a review into the last few hours before an examination is not a winning strategy.

We've stressed studying for an examination, but we have really been writing about studying for mastery. Mastering something doesn't mean that you will not "forget" it, though in a sense if you have really mastered something, it is always with you. When faced with a problem in statistics years after you have studied the subject, you may feel that you remember nothing. But after a few minutes of working on the problem, it will all come back. Things that you have mastered—that you have studied well—become part of you. They never leave you, and they allow you to understand and appreciate your world in a deeper and more knowing way.

UNDERLINING, HIGHLIGHTING, AND OUTLINING TEXTBOOKS

Most students underline or highlight textbooks or make notes. These are good ways to prepare for review. Note-taking in particular, if done right, provides for recitation. Because these techniques are so important to studying from textbooks, we have a special section on them.

Underlining and Highlighting

A typical practice of poor students is to sit down with a book in front of them and just read away in a listless manner. When they see something they think is important, they underline or highlight it. They do this without surveying or asking questions. The result is a hit-or-miss selection of passages, something that reflects a chance judgment rather than any overall organization of the material. If you do this, you are stuck with what you have done. You may think that you have underscored the important points, but you have probably not only missed some, but you may have selected others that are of minor importance. You can correct this somewhat by checking when you review to make sure you have hit the major points.

Incidentally, if you are buying a secondhand textbook, make sure you get one that has not been underlined or highlighted. If you can't find a book that isn't marked up, buy a new one. The handicap of being subject to someone else's underlining is far too serious to be worth the amount of money you save by buying a used book.

Underlining and highlighting have their place. Some people find them useful, and others do not. But if they are to be useful to you, they must be done wisely at the right time and according to a plan. The plan is this: First survey what you are going to read. Then ask yourself questions and try to answer those questions as you read. *In this first reading it is better not to underline or highlight.* You won't really know what is important until you have grasped the whole. As your questions are answered or as you think that you spot main ideas and important details, make a checkmark in the margin. The next time you read, read for the main ideas, important details, and technical terms. It is these you will want to underline or highlight.

Even on the second, careful reading, don't underline or highlight sentences as you read them. After you have read one or two paragraphs, go back and decide what it is you are going to mark. As a guide, use your checkmarks in the margin. If they don't designate the main points, you can ignore them.

Don't underline or highlight whole sentences. Many of the words in a sentence that contains an important idea are unimportant. Leave these out when you underline. (We know that it is easier just to move the marker across the page, but that's the point. Anything that's easy to do does not allow you to be an active student.) Underline only the words or phrases that are essential. If you do this, you will be able to pick up only the important words easily. That will force you to reconstruct the rest. On pages 85–86, you will find an example of good underlining. Look at this example carefully and try to figure out why we underlined things the way we did.

If you follow these guidelines, you will not underline or highlight as much as most students do. On the average, a half-dozen or so words per paragraph will do the trick, though, of course, how much you mark your textbook in this way depends upon the material you are studying.

Taking Reading Notes

Taking notes as you read your textbook is one way to be active in the learning process. If you write down in short form what the author says, you make it part of your own mental processes. You can't fool yourself into believing that you have really been studying when your mind has been elsewhere.

Methods of Outlining

One way of arranging the information of a chapter for ease of studying is to take notes in outline form. How do you go about outlining? First, use whatever clues the author gives you for an outline. If there are headings, you can get the skeleton of your outline from these. Don't just copy them, however. Most headings are not sentences; they are just a few key words. Sometimes converting them into full but short sentences helps. (For example, for the heading for this section you might have written, "Here are some methods of Outlining." Or better yet, "Here are some ways to outline.") Sometimes, in order to make a sentence out of the heading for a section, you will have to read the complete section first.

Your outline should be orderly. There are two ways to achieve this. One way is to indent one order of statement under another so that the main state-

Underlining a Textbook

Here is an example of underlining to pick out the main points (from C. R. McConnell and S. L. Brue, *Economics: Principles, Problems, and Policies,* 11th ed., The McGraw-Hill Companies, New York, 1990, pp. 40–41. This material was reproduced with permission of The McGraw-Hill Companies.).

Extensive Use of Capital Goods

All modern economies—whether they approximate the capitalist, socialist, or communist ideology—are based upon an advanced technology and the extensive use of capital goods. Under pure capitalism it is competition, coupled with freedom of choice and the desire to further one's self-interest, which provides the means for achieving technological advance. The capitalistic framework is felt to be highly effective in harnessing incentives to develop new products and improved techniques of production. Why? Because the monetary rewards derived therefrom accrue directly to the innovator. Pure capitalism therefore presupposes the extensive use and relatively rapid development of complex capital goods: tools, machinery, large-scale factories, and facilities for storage, transportation, and marketing.

Why are the existence of an advanced technology and the extensive use of capital goods important? Because the most direct method of producing a product is usually the least efficient.[2] Even Robinson Crusoe avoided the inefficiencies of direct production in favor of "roundabout production." It would be ridiculous for a farmer—even a backyard farmer—to go at production with bare hands. Obviously, it pays huge dividends in terms of more efficient production and, therefore, a more abundant output, to fashion tools of production, that is, capital equipment, to aid in the productive process. There is a better way of getting water out of a well than to dive in after it!

But there is a catch involved. As we recall our discussion of the production possibilities curve and the basic nature of the economizing problem, it is evident that, with full employment and full production, resources must be diverted from the production of consumer goods in order to be used in the production of capital goods. We must currently tighten our belts as consumers in order to free resources for the production of capital goods which will increase productive efficiency and permit us to have a greater output of consumer goods at some future date.

---

[2]Remember that consumer goods satisfy wants directly, while capital goods do so indirectly through the more efficient production of consumer goods.

Underlining a Textbook (*Continued*)

Specialization

The extent to which <u>society relies upon specialization</u> is astounding. The vast majority of <u>consumers produce virtually none of the goods and services they consume</u> and, conversely, consume little or nothing of what they produce. The hammer-shop laborer who spends his lifetime stamping out parts for jet engines may never "consume" an airplane trip. The assembly-line worker who devotes eight hours a day to the installation of windows in Camaros may own a Honda. Few households seriously consider any extensive production of their own food, shelter, and clothing. Many farmers sell their milk to the local dairy and then buy margarine at the Podunk general store. Society learned long ago that self-sufficiency breeds inefficiency. The jack-of-all-trades may be a very colorful individual, but is certainly lacking in efficiency.

<u>In what</u> specific <u>ways</u> might human specialization—*<u>the division of labor</u>*—enhance <u>productive efficiency</u>? First, specialization permits individuals to <u>take advantage</u> of existing <u>differences</u> in their <u>abilities and skills</u>. If caveman A is strong, swift afoot, and accurate with a spear, and caveman B is weak and slow, but patient, this distribution of talents can be most efficiently utilized by making A a hunter and B a fisherman. Second, even if the abilities of A and B are identical, specialization may prove to be advantageous. Why? Because by . . . .

ments are at the left margin and subsidiary statements begin slightly to the right. The other way of structuring your outline is to use a consistent system of lettering and numbering the different levels of entries. There are several ways of doing that, and, if you have one way that works, there is no need to change. If you don't, try using Roman numerals (I, II, III, . . .) for the highest-level headings, capital letters (A, B, C, . . .) for the second level, Arabic numerals (1, 2, 3, . . .) for the third, lowercase letters (a, b, c, . . .) for the fourth level, and lowercase Roman numerals (i, ii, iii, . . .) for the lowest level. More often than not, the methods of indenting and numbering and lettering are combined, as in the sample outline on pages 87–89.

Outlining from Books

Here is an outline from this book, Chapter 4, "The Art of Reading." It illustrates how you might outline material found in a textbook.

I. Reading well and liking to read go together.
II. If you are deficient in reading you will:
  A. Move your lips or vocalize when you read.
  B. Read each word one by one.
  C. Find many unfamiliar words while reading.
  D. Backtrack and reread what you have just read.
  E. Read everything at the same rate and in the same way.
  F. Not understand what you have read.
III. Reading with a purpose.
  A. Skimming.
    1. Look for signposts.
      a. Look for headings.
      b. If there are no headings read the first sentences of paragraphs.
    2. Skimming is the first step in studying.
  B. Read to get the main idea.
    1. Finding the main idea.
      a. At different levels: chapters, sections, paragraphs.
      b. Paragraph contains a single topic.
        i. Topic sentence usually at beginning of paragraph.
        ii. But sometimes it occurs elsewhere in paragraph.
    2. Main idea not necessarily whole sentence.
      a. May be the principal clause of a sentence.
      b. May need to be boiled down in your own words.
      c. Often can throw away qualifiers.
    3. Sometimes main idea not expressed, only implied.
  C. Extracting important details.
    1. Details often examples—particularly in science.
    2. Often a matter of judgment.
    3. Make identifying them habitual—without thinking about it.
  D. Reading for pleasure.
    1. The more you read for pleasure, the better reader you will be.
    2. Read for pleasure in all the different ways you read to learn.
  E. Evaluate what you read—examine your own beliefs.
  F. Expand what you read to apply to situations not mentioned by author.

Outlining from Books (*Continued*)

IV. Using your eyes.
    A. Eye movements.
        1. Saccades are quick movements broken by brief pauses.
        2. Pauses are fixations.
            a. Fixations last one-quarter to one-fifth of a second.
            b. Read during fixations.
        3. Very little difference between good and poor readers in speed of saccades.
        4. Good readers fix on the average only once every three words.
        5. Poor readers make more regressive saccades.
        6. Good readers make a single return movement at the end of a line; poor readers overshoot or under-shoot.
    B. Improving eye movements.
        1. Eye movements in reading are automatic or reflexive.
            a. Can't improve them much consciously.
            b. Major emphasis now upon improving mental habits of reading.
            c. Keeping a record of reading speed helps to increase speed.
        2. Upper limit to reading speed about 900 words a minute.
        3. Most students read at a rate of 200 to 300 words a minute.
            a. That rate can be pushed quite a bit higher.
            b. As you do so, your eye movements will automatically improve.
V. How to improve your reading.
    A. Building a vocabulary.
        1. Lots of new words encountered in college.
        2. Good vocabulary mark of a good student and good reader.
        3. Be on the lookout for new words.
        4. Use the dictionary often.
            a. A good dictionary is essential.
            b. In looking up a word, find out its meaning in the context in which you found it.
        5. Use vocabulary cards to improve a poor vocabulary.
        6. Distinguish between general and technical terms.
            a. May need glossary or special dictionary for technical terms.
            b. Sometimes half or more of the subject matter may be in knowing what technical terms mean.
        7. How to dissect words.
            a. Many words consist of roots, prefixes, and suffixes.
            b. Knowing the meaning of commonly used prefixes and suffixes may help you guess the meaning of new words correctly.
            c. Many English words are built on Latin and Greek roots.

Outlining from Books (*Continued*)

B. Learning to read faster.
1. Very few people read at their maximum rate.
2. Reading faster requires practice.
   a. For practice to be effective, you must know whether you are improving or not.
   b. Therefore, you must keep a record of how fast you are reading.
      i. Devote a special period each day to practice at fast reading.
      ii. Use the same kind of material every day.
      iii. Use the same format.
      iv. Use material of moderate difficulty.
      v. Time yourself.
      vi. Count the words and calculate your reading rate.
      vii. Make a chart or graph of your reading rate.
      viii. Be sure you are not sacrificing comprehension for speed.
3. If your reading is exceptionally slow or you don't improve, you will need help.
4. Practice skimming.
   a. There are two kinds of skimming.
      i. Searching for key words.
      ii. Searching for key words and phrases on your initial survey.
   b. Use browsing for secondary or less-important reading.

Content of Notes

Your notes should contain the main ideas and important details. Be sure to put enough into your notes so that you can understand them later. If, for example, you are outlining a section in a physics text on the idea of the "wave front," don't just write down "Huygens's Principle." Tell what Huygens's Principle is. You might write, "Huygens's Principle: Every point on a wave front is a point source for waves generated in the direction of the wave's propagation."

Write as legibly as you can. Even people who have good handwriting get hurried when they take notes, and they can't read what they wrote later on. (If your handwriting is hard to read anyway, make a special effort to improve it when you take textbook notes. With practice, your writing should become clear enough for instructors to read it without difficulty. While almost no teacher wants to admit it, clear handwriting is probably worth some points on an examination.)

When Not to Outline

Making outline notes of textbook material helps you understand and remember what you read. However, there are some subjects for which outline notes are not appropriate. You would not want to outline a foreign language text. Such texts consist of a mixture of grammatical rules, vocabulary, and sentences to be translated. In the physical sciences, your textbook is likely to be almost in outline form to begin with, and it is hardly worth your time to copy the outline. Instead, you would do better to focus on silent recitation or written recitation as you read. When you read literature, you do not read in order to understand particular facts or theories; you read in order to interpret. Rather than putting what you read into your own words, think about what the author is saying. Think about why the author wrote the essay or story the way he or she did. Be alert to the imagery and be ready to interpret any symbols you may come across. Some people make notes in margins; others keep a notebook for written comments.

The first time you read a story, don't make notes. On the rereading you may want to take notes or make comments. A useful form for making notes is to cast them in the form of questions. Why did the characters react as they did? In some literature textbooks you will find questions of this sort included to help you understand what you are reading.

In reading stories or novels, be on the lookout for seemingly superficial details but which prove to be central to the understanding of characters or to the mood the author wishes to convey. Watch for allusions. Good writers often make allusions to classical mythology or religious themes. *Do you know where they come from?* If you have a demanding teacher, you will be expected to know.

Not all literature is in the form of fiction, drama, or narrative poetry. You will be expected to read some essays, and you may be asked to read works like Darwin's *Origin of Species* or Marx's *Das Kapital* not just for the information they contain but because of the enormous influence they have had and because of the *way in which they were written*. Essays and such important works as these are not like textbooks. They are discursive. That means that the writers let their minds wander over a vast landscape instead of merely telling you something you don't know. So often these works need to be read in the way in which you would read stories. Ask yourself: "Why did the author say things in exactly that way? Is there anything in the work that reflects the author's personal life?" In brief, you need to read such works in their literary and historical contexts.

But—and this is a big but—you are expected to know what the literary works are about. It is a good idea to write summaries of them, summaries that incorporate something of your own views. That brings us to our next point.

Writing Summaries

Summaries are helpful for almost anything you read. They are useful for textbooks, particularly those that do not include chapter summaries themselves. However, for textbooks, don't try to write a summary until you have mastered the material. Summaries should be as brief as possible, but they should contain all the essential information.

If you write a summary of a story, be sure that it is more than just a bare recital of the narrative. Characterize the people in the story and include your reactions to them. Try to capture the atmosphere of the story, the feeling it evokes in you. Comment on any irony, imagery, and symbolism that you may have come across.

Taking Notes from History Texts

History texts often have a unique organization, and it isn't just that things are arranged chronologically. Modern texts and history instructors tend to place less emphasis on dates than they did in the past, but you still had better be able to place the Treaty of Ghent or the founding of the Federal Reserve System in their right times. The easiest way to do this is to get the dates *right*.

The typical organization of a history text is to divide it into some spans of time that have natural significance. The history of France (or western Europe, for that matter) has a kind of continuity from 1815 and the Congress of Vienna to the revolutions of 1848 and, in France, the establishment of the Second Republic. So after you have surveyed and read your text, you might make notes by blocking off several pages in your notebook to be devoted to the period from 1815 to 1848. Do your textbook notes on the left side (the even-numbered page) and leave room on the right side (the odd-numbered page) for lecture notes that correspond. Then you can indicate the significant events, ideas, and people in a sensible order. Since modern history courses stress social, intellectual, and technological history as well as the traditional political history, you might rule off your note pages into parallel columns with these issues as headings. This way you can see, for example, how the development of railroads and industry paralleled changes in where people lived and the kinds of clothes they wore as well as the politics of the time.

Example of a Summary

Here is a summary of Chapter 4, "The Art of Reading." Compare the statements in this summary with the headings and main ideas in the chapter. Also, compare it with the outline on pages 87–89 to see how an outline and a summary differ.

In college you will have to do more reading than you have ever done, and you will need to work at doing better at it. When you read better, you will like it more. If you move your lips when you read, read word by word, find a lot of unfamiliar words, backtrack, read everything the same way, or fail to understand what you read, you are a poor reader and will need to improve.

There are different purposes in reading and different ways to read. Skimming is one way to read. In one kind of skimming you look for headings and subheadings. Another way to skim is to search for critical words. We also read to get the main idea. The main idea of a paragraph is the topic sentence, often found at the beginning of the paragraph. In looking for the main idea, don't look for whole sentences. Pick out the key words and phrases. Sometimes the author will not state the main idea but only imply it. This happens often in literary texts. Sometimes you will want to read to extract important details. Important ideas are often examples, particularly in scientific texts. Often you have to use your judgment to find important details. When you read for pleasure, you will want to suit your reading to your purpose, just as you do when you read to learn. Keep an active attitude toward reading; evaluate what you read.

When you read, your eyes move in a series of quick movements broken by brief pauses. The movements are called "saccades," and the pauses are "fixations." The pauses last about one-quarter to one-fifth of a second, and they occupy about 90 percent of the total time in reading. There are also regressive movements. These occur more often in poor readers. Another difference between good and poor readers is in the return movement at the end of a line. Poor readers overshoot or undershoot.

The best way to improve your eye movements in reading is to improve your mental habits. You can't read faster than 900 words a minute, but since the typical student reads only 200 to 300 words a minute, there is a lot of room for improvement. To improve your reading, you need to build your vocabulary. You will learn many new technical terms in college, and you must pay attention to these. Use your dictionary fre-

Example of a Summary (*Continued*)

quently. If you have serious trouble with vocabulary, use vocabulary cards. For technical terms you will need to consult glossaries and technical dictionaries. Learn to dissect words into prefixes, roots, and suffixes. Know the meaning of as many prefixes and suffixes as you can.

Practice timing yourself at reading. Do this every day with the same kind of material. Make a chart or graph of the results to see if you are actually improving. If your reading rate is very poor or if you don't improve, you will need to find special help. Practice skimming as well as reading.

While it is not strictly a note-taking concern for a history class, you should be sure that you can use and interpret maps effectively. Study the maps in your textbook and perhaps make sketches of them so that you can impress them upon your mind. On an examination, you may be given a blank map and asked to indicate certain features on it. You could be given a blank map of, say, North America and asked to indicate the limits of the French and British settlements on the eve of the French and Indian War. Or you could be given a map of the Atlantic Ocean and asked to diagram the elements of the slave trade. Even if there are no maps on the exam, maps are a good way to help you retain information that you may be asked to produce. For example, it is much easier to remember that the provinces of Alsace and Lorraine were ceded by France to Germany after the War of 1870 if you know roughly where Alsace and Lorraine are. Otherwise you are forced to memorize a statement that has no real meaning for you.

Summarizing a Chapter

The time to recite what you have read in this chapter is now. If you haven't already made an outline, do it now. Then run back through the chapter to make sure you haven't missed something. Write a summary using your outline. We've provided a summary of Chapter 4 on pages 92–93. It is somewhat long, but it is better to err on the side of being too long than to leave something out.

Taking Examinations

6

If you believe in miracles, then you may think that you can pass examinations without studying for them. For most of us, however, that's not possible. After all, the main purpose of examinations is to determine how effectively you have studied. If you have followed all the rules for effective studying, you should be ready for an examination and have no need of miracles. In this chapter we offer a few additional ideas for taking examinations.

PREPARING FOR EXAMINATIONS

You all know the rule: Be prepared. Be prepared for the *kind* of examination you are going to take and for *all* the possible questions, not just for some of them. Master the subject thoroughly and organize it well. Be in good physical condition, rested, and in a confident frame of mind.

The Final Review

If you have kept up with your studying, preparing for an exam is mainly a matter of review. The final review should be an intensive one. You will go over your textbook notes and your lecture notes looking for main ideas. Review any lists of technical terms, dates, etc.

A review is just that—a review. It should be an effort to recall things you have already learned. If you are reading material for the first time just before an exam, you had better hope for a miracle. You are in deep trouble. If the exam is easy and the material not too difficult, you might be able to skate by. But if this is the case, then you should be able to get an A on an easy exam; getting a respectable B won't do.

In some subjects you may want to make a set of review notes. These can be of two kinds. They can be a condensation of your detailed notes, or they can be compilations of all the things you found difficult, are apt to forget, or need to commit to memory.

Schedule of Reviews

Surprisingly, it is easy to overestimate the time you will need for review. If you have kept up with your work, reviewing for an exam will not take a lot of time. Just be sure to allow enough time to cover *everything*. Keep your review sessions short. When your attention begins to wander, do something else for a while.

Make a definite plan for review, just as you schedule your regular hours of study. For the week prior to your final exams, revise your regular study schedule to accommodate reviewing. You may need to cut down on some of your free time, but don't cut into it too deeply; you still need to relax. You won't need to give up some free time if you have been following a good study regime.

This brings up the subject of cramming. All of us at one time or another have boasted about some cram session. We've all heard the stories about staying up all night and living on black coffee. Most students do more talking than cramming, but this kind of frantic, disorganized studying does occur, and it is inefficient and even harmful. Going without food, sleep, and rest is physically draining; if you have been doing that, it will take a superhuman effort of will to do your best at exam time. If you are not in good shape, your judgment will be affected; you may not even know whether answers you have given on an exam are right or wrong. It doesn't take pep pills to disorient you. Students who have spent all night studying sometimes write gibberish thinking that they are making sense.

It goes without saying (but we'll say it anyway) that taking an exam after a night's session on alcohol or drugs is about the worst thing you can do. Students sometimes try to calm themselves down or try to get to sleep by taking alcohol or drugs. You may feel a little better when you finally get to sleep, but you will feel awful at exam time. And since you will have residual alcohol or whatever in your bloodstream, your mental efficiency will be impaired.

Organize your life so that you can live as normally as possible during exam time. Get regular meals, sleep, and recreation. Keep up with all your subjects. You may not have much to offer in a bull session on cramming, but you will be way ahead on your exams.

How to Review

Emphasize recitation. Keep your rereading to a minimum. Go at the job chapter by chapter, topic by topic. First try to recall the main ideas without referring to your notes or the book. For each main heading in a chapter, do the same thing. First recall the main points. Then check. If you can't remember something or can't understand or explain a point, go back to the book and reread the passage covering it. If you attempt to do more rereading than this at once, you will lose sight of the important points.

It is easy to fall into the trap of trying to outguess the instructor. Don't try to guess what the instructor's favorite topics are. Your instructor knows that you will try to do that and will very likely not put proportionally more questions about a certain topic on a test even if the topic is a personal favorite. Yes, it may be helpful to see prior exams (many instructors keep them on file in the library), but don't rule out unpleasant surprises. Keep a balance in the material you study. That way you won't end up saying those famous sad words, "I studied the wrong things."

If you prepare for anything that could be asked instead of concentrating on a few topics, you will be able to deal with anything that turns up. As you review, turn what you review into questions. How would you word a question about this topic? One way that you can outguess the instructor is to take advantage of any hints, direct or indirect, about the way the questions will be asked. Most instructors will give you some idea about the format of the test—what portion will be objective in nature and how many subjective (essay) questions to expect.

Types of Exams

Most exams are either objective or essay. Objective exams do not require you to write. All you do is decide whether a statement is true or false, decide which of several statements is true, or decide how statements should be matched. Objective exams focus on your ability to recognize the right answers when you see them, not your ability to recall or organize the information you have learned.

Essay exams on the other hand require you to recall what you have learned and to organize it and present it in a coherent way. In science and mathematics classes you may be given problems to solve. Like essays, problems stress your ability to recall rather than recognize information. That is true even when the problems are presented in multiple-choice or some other objective format. If you aren't going to guess the correct answer, then you must recall how to solve the problem and then work it out.

There are some types of questions that fall between objective questions and essay questions. These are usually called completion questions in which you are required to fill in the correct word or phrase to make a statement true. Sometimes you will be asked to identify or describe something briefly. These kinds of questions do not require you to organize a lot of information, but they do ask for recall.

Because objective exams require that you select only the right answer, many students don't prepare as thoroughly for them as they do for essay exams. This is a mistake. Most objective exams are graded on the curve. Thus all students have the same advantage, and, if you do only an average preparation, that is where you will end up—in the middle.

Many students think that objective exam questions are picky, that they emphasize trivial details. If you feel this way, consider the role of details in an essay. Well-chosen details serve to develop and support the points of an essay. If you can enrich the answers in an essay with details, the instructor is going to believe that you really do know what you are talking about. The point is that details are important in either kind of test question.

The really important difference between essay and objective exams lies in organization. Essay questions require you to do more work because you must organize your answers. They don't require you to know more, but the organization of an essay into a coherent form is difficult for many students. If essay questions give you a hard time, practice by making up your own questions and then write the answers. (Or ask a study partner to ask you questions.) You might ask your instructor to critique some of your efforts. Most instructors would be happy to do this because it shows that you have initiative and that you are serious about succeeding.

TEST ANXIETY

Test anxiety is a real phenomenon. We see students so upset on test day that they can't make it to class. Others sit in class with tears in their eyes or with a rash or such a bad case of the shakes that they can't write legibly. What is the best way to avoid such adverse reactions? Be prepared. Of course, even the best-prepared students are occasionally going to have rumbling guts at test time, but the chances are that they are going to be better off than their classmates who are not as well prepared. We have always felt that it takes one exam to figure out an instructor. If you do well on the first exam, then you can assume that your preparation is adequate. If you don't do as well as you expected to do on the first exam, then you need to reassess your methods of preparing for tests. If the course will require you to spend more time in preparation, you will need to revise your schedule accordingly.

In addition to being well prepared, there are a few other things you can do to reduce your anxiety. Try to take care of your body before the test. Get to the exam location well before the test starts. Avoid being rushed. Being rushed only makes your anxiety worse. Spend a few minutes before the exam in small talk (not about the test) or read the campus newspaper or do anything that will put you in a relaxed mood. A last-minute frantic review while waiting for the exam to be handed out will only increase your panic because by doing this you are telling yourself that there are some things you don't know.

Don't get rattled during the test. Have a strategy for taking a test. We recommend that for the first minute or so, you merely read the test—don't write anything. In that time you will likely see something that you know very well; do that first. That will alleviate some anxiety for you to know that you have a good start. As you work on the rest of the test, don't spend too much time on any one question early in the time allotted. Give yourself a chance to answer all the questions you can as soon as you can, and leave the more difficult questions for the end when you should have time to consider your answers. When you do this, be sure that you place your answers in the correct spot on an answer sheet. Answers misaligned on a Scantron sheet are scored as wrong despite your intentions.

You will find that, as you gain confidence in your ability to cope with the stress of an exam, the tendency to fall apart will gradually diminish. Above all *don't blame poor preparation on test anxiety*. Be prepared.

If, in spite of being prepared and well rested before an exam, you are still crippled by anxiety, you will need to look for help. Many counseling services offer special sessions on how to reduce test anxiety. If your college does not have such a service, at least discuss your problem with a counselor. Panic before examinations, even when you are well prepared, is a symptom of an underlying problem. You must seek help.

TAKING OBJECTIVE EXAMINATIONS

Here are some of the things you should do when you are faced with an objective examination:

1. Survey. When you pick up an objective exam, flip through the pages to see how long it is and how many questions are on it. Note how many questions there are of each type—true–false, multiple-choice, matching—so that you can determine how to divide your time among them.

2. Read directions carefully. Make sure you know what you are supposed to do. Indicate your answers exactly the way the directions tell you to. If you don't, you may be in trouble.

3. Be sure you understand the scoring rules. If there is no penalty for guessing, you have nothing to lose by trying to answer every question. If, on the other hand, points are subtracted for wrong answers, then you are penalized for guessing and you must follow a more conservative plan.

If, on a true-false test, the instructor arrives at your score by subtracting the number wrong from the number correct, you should guess and try to answer every question because, on average, you will answer right more often than wrong if you know *anything* about the material at all. But if the instructor corrects for this taking the number right minus *two* times the number wrong, you should be very careful about guessing. Guess only when you have a strong feeling that your answer is correct.

Whatever you do, read the instructor's directions. If the instructor says, "There is no penalty for guessing" or "Don't guess because wrong answers will be penalized," adjust what you do accordingly. Don't hesitate to ask for clarification about penalties if the situation is not clear to you.

4. Answer easy questions first. Read some of the questions until you recognize one that you can answer easily. Answer that one first. If you have to stop and think, put a check mark in the margin (if you are allowed to put marks on the test) and go on to the next question. Come back to the hard ones after you have done all the easy ones. Don't get bogged down on one time-consuming question at the expense of the ones that you might have answered easily. Keep an eye on the time and know how much time is left. Apportion your time sensibly so that you can answer as many of the hard questions as possible.

This is particularly good advice for an objective test in which the questions are problems that must be worked out such as on many science and math tests.

5. *Place the question in context.* As you read the questions, remember their context. Ask yourself how this question ought to be answered in light of your textbook and the lectures. Identify the source, if possible. Don't answer the question based on your own personal opinion or what has been said in some other class you might be taking. Even if you think the instructor or the textbook is wrong, it is still your job to show that you know what the correct answer is from the point of view of the course you are taking.

Some Tips on True-False Questions

True-false questions consist of some simple statements that relate two things. "Roses are red" is not likely to be a real question because the statement lacks a qualifier. A more likely question would be "All roses are red" which includes the qualifier "all." Instructors are interested in knowing whether or not you know when and under what circumstances a statement is true. So typical true-false questions normally contain a qualifier.

Analyze Qualifiers   Qualifiers are very important in a true-false statement. Here are some important qualifiers you may see:

All, most, some, few, none, no

Always, usually, sometimes, rarely, never

Great, much, little, no, none

More, equal, less

Good, bad

You can test qualifiers by substituting another in the same group for the one you see in the given statement. If your substitution makes more sense than the original, then the statement is probably false. If your substitution does not make more sense, the statement is likely true. For example, suppose the statement is "Some roses are red." The alternatives are:

All roses are red.

Most roses are red.

Few roses are red.

No roses are red.

The two extreme statements are clearly not true. You may have some question about "Most . . ." and "Few . . . ," but even if one of them is true, then "Some . . ." would also have to be true. None of the substitutions makes a better statement than the original, so it must be true.

Don't spend too much time on qualifiers, however. Take the time to test them only if you think you are being misled by the one in the question.

Pick Out Key Words   Even more important than analyzing qualifiers is finding the key word or phrase in a question. It is the word or group of words upon which the truth or falsity of the statement depends. It is difficult, but not impossible, to construct a true statement using the qualifiers "no," "never," "always," or "every," but you need to judge each statement in light of what you know. The exercise on page 102 will give you some practice in identifying key words and phrases.

Finally, don't try to guess your way through a true-false test by trying to find a pattern to the sequence of answers. It's unlikely there is any.

Answering Multiple-Choice Questions

Multiple-choice questions are true-false questions arranged in groups. A lead phrase combines with three or more alternate endings to make different statements. The directions almost always say, "Choose the *best* answer." It is possible that more than one answer may be correct, but only one is best. For example:

Roses most often grow:

a. on bushes.

b. on trees.

c. in winter.

d. in summer.

By checking the key words "most often," we see that both *a* and *d* are true, but roses also grow in spring and fall. The best answer then is *a*.

Exercise in Key Words

Here is a list of true-false questions that you might encounter early on in any introductory psychology course. It is designed to point to commonly held misconceptions. The answer to each of these true-false questions is "false." However, what you need to do is to pick out the key words that make them false. When you are finished, check your selections with the ones listed below.

Key Words

1. Geniuses are always neurotic.   _____
2. You can accurately tell what someone is thinking from facial expression.   _____
3. Cats can see in total darkness.   _____
4. There is a clear distinction between normal people and emotionally disturbed people.   _____
5. If people were always honest, we would get along with one another better.   _____
6. Your IQ is completely determined by heredity.   _____
7. Psychology can never be objective.   _____
8. Stuttering is usually the result of poor speech training.   _____
9. If you practice enough, you can read anything at the rate of 1000 words a minute.   _____
10. Darwin was the first person to advocate a theory of evolution.   _____
11. With statistics you can prove anything.   _____
12. Urban legends always have some basis in fact.   _____
13. It has been proven that animals can sense a coming earthquake.   _____
14. It is possible to classify everyone as either extroverted or introverted.   _____
15. Slow learners remember better what they learn than do fast learners.   _____
16. You can size up a person very well in an interview.   _____
17. All people are neurotic.   _____
18. Studying mathematics will necessarily make you a better thinker.   _____
19. A psychologist is someone trained to psychoanalyze people.   _____
20. A first experience at intercourse can never make a girl pregnant.   _____

The key words for each question are as follows: (1) always, (2) accurately, (3) total, (4) clear, (5) always, better, (6) completely, (7) never, (8) usually, (9) anything, (10) first person, (11) prove, anything, (12) always, (13) proven, (14) everyone, (15) better, (16) very well, (17) all, (18) necessarily, (19) psychoanalyze, (20) never.

Many times the correct answer is a relative matter, not one of absolute truth or falsity. For this reason, you will want to adopt a strategy of elimination. Take, for example, the following question:

The American philosopher most influential in the philosophy of education is:

a. William James.

b. Bertrand Russell.

c. John Dewey.

d. Nathaniel Hawthorne.

If you remember that Hawthorne was the author of *The Scarlet Letter,* you will know that he was not, strictly speaking, a philosopher, and he can easily be eliminated. The other three are all philosophers, and unless you know something about philosophy and the philosophy of education, you will have a hard time arriving at the *best* answer. The key words can help here. They are "American," "philosophy of education," and "most." Bertrand Russell was British; you can eliminate him. So you have to choose between William James and John Dewey. Both wrote on education, so the key word in choosing between them is "most." John Dewey is undoubtedly the choice the instructor had in mind, because he was and still is the towering influence in American education.

Once you have made your decision, mark the answer and go on to the next question. If you can't make up your mind between a couple of plausible alternatives, place a check mark at the side and leave the question until you have answered the easier ones. Many times you can get hints from the other questions on a test, so read every question carefully and then go back to the more difficult questions. If time is running out and there is no penalty for guessing, guess. Don't leave questions unanswered in these circumstances.

Answering Matching Questions

You may apply similar strategies to matching questions. Read all the items to be matched so that you know all the possibilities. Then take the first item on the left and read down the items on the right until you find the one that you're sure is the best match. If you are not certain, leave the item and go on to the next one. Fill in only those you are certain of. That way, you will reduce the number of possibilities when you must decide on the difficult matches.

Some matching questions consist only of words and brief phrases to be matched. Others contain whole clauses similar to those in true-false or multiple-choice statements. If that is the case, try to spot the key words.

Answering Completion Questions

One kind of question used fairly often in large classes is the completion question. Completion questions provide statements with key words of phrases left out. In answering this kind of question, choose your words carefully. The instructor probably has something very specific in mind. A single word is probably required, but if you think that more than one is absolutely required, write them down. Try to come up with the very best wording so that you will get full credit, not half. But if you can't think of the exact answer, write something down. Instructors seldom penalize for guessing on completion questions, and, while you may look a little silly to the grader by giving such a far out answer, you might have the right idea.

Finishing the Exam

We've told you to answer the easy questions first on an objective exam and then go back to answer the hard ones. Before you work on the harder questions, note how much time you have left and allocate it among the remaining questions. Leave some time for a final glance over the exam. You may spot some careless mistakes.

When you reread your examination, you will be tempted to change some of your answers. If you feel strongly that an answer is wrong and should be changed, change it. If, however, you had a hard time making up your mind between two answers, don't change the answer you wrote the first time. If you are guessing, your first answer is more likely to be right. Change your answer only if you are reasonably sure that your first answer is wrong. It is a terrible thing to be changing right answers to wrong ones at the end of the exam.

TAKING ESSAY EXAMINATIONS

In essay exams your work consists of writing organized, precise, and concise answers to questions rather than reading questions and trying to figure out the right answers. At the one extreme these questions will require you to write something quite specific. At the other extreme they will ask you to "discuss" some general issue in order to indicate the amount of thought you have given to what you have studied. Most essay exams will be a mixture of these two types. There are also short-answer questions. These require a slightly different strategy, and we have a word to say about them shortly. First, however, we give you some general principles that apply to all essay exams.

Planning Your Time

Planning and allocating time are even more important in essay exams than in objective exams. Students are likely to know more than they have time to write, and it is easy to get carried away on a subject you know a lot about. If you're not careful, you will spend too much time on some questions and give others short shrift. That will probably lower your grade because the grader will likely give all answers equal weight. Read through the whole exam first and decide how much time you can afford to spend on each question. If you have a choice of which questions to answer, choose the ones you want to tackle at the beginning. That decision should depend on a number of things— how much you know about a particular topic, how hard the question is, and, above all, how much you would have to write.

Following Directions

The key words in an essay exam are in the instructions. They are such words as "list," "illustrate," "compare," "outline," "state," "discuss," and so on. The instructor chooses such words carefully and expects you to do what you are told. Students who aren't prepared as well as they should be are tempted to write around a subject—to tell everything they know about a subject regardless of whether their response is relevant to the question or not. This is not only a waste of time, but it tells the grader that either you didn't know what you were writing about or that you didn't understand the question. Graders ignore what isn't relevant, and tough instructors may even deduct for evading the question. Stick as close to the directions as you can. If you're told to list, do that. Don't illustrate or discuss. If you're told to compare, be sure you do that. On pages 106–107 is a table that lists the key words in the instructions for essay exams and explains how to interpret them.

Organizing Your Answers

A significant difference between a good essay and a poor one is organization. The best way to make sure that your answer will be coherent and organized is to outline your answer first. When you are sure you understand what the question is about, decide what points you will make and sketch these in out-

Important Words in Essay Questions

Here are some of the words that provide the critical instructions for answering essay questions. We've provided a brief summary of what each tells you to do.

Compare
Look for similarities and differences between the things mentioned (e.g., "Compare the U.S. and Confederate Constitutions").

Contrast
Stress the dissimilarities.

Criticize
Make a judgment about the item in question. Stress the deficiencies (e.g., "Criticize Paul Valéry's views on the poet's language").

Define
Provide a concise and accurate definition of what is called for.

Describe
Mention the chief characteristics of a situation or retell the essential features of a story (e.g., "Describe France on the eve of the revolution," or "Describe Conrad's *Heart of Darkness*").

Diagram
Provide a drawing, chart, or plan.

Discuss
Be analytical. Give reasons pro and con.

Evaluate
Provide both positive and negative sides of the topic (e.g., "Evaluate the role of Disraeli in forming the modern Conservative Party").

Explain
Give reasons for what is asked for. Provide the causes (e.g., "Explain the reasons for the notion of penetrance in population genetics").

Illustrate
Use examples. Or, where appropriate, provide a diagram or figure.

Interpret
Translate, solve, or comment on a subject, usually giving your judgment about it.

Important Words in Essay Questions (*Continued*)

Justify
Provide the reasons for your conclusions or for the statement made in the question (e.g., "Justify Henry Clay's interpretation of the Constitution").

List
Provide an itemized list. The items should be numbered.

Outline
Organize your answer into main points and subordinate points. While it is not necessary that your answer be in outline form, it helps to prepare it that way.

Prove
Provide factual evidence or, where appropriate, a logical or mathematical proof.

Relate
Show the connection between the things mentioned in the question. Note that this does not mean to compare, so if you are asked to relate the American and French revolutions, you are not to compare them but to show how one influenced the other.

Review
Provide a summary, usually a critical one. A review usually also implies commenting on important aspects of the question.

Summarize
Provide a summary, usually without comment or criticism.

Trace
Describe the progress of some historical event or, where appropriate, describe the causes of some event.

---

line form. Then use this outline as a guide to writing the answer. After you are through, you can cross out your outline so that it won't be viewed as part of your answer. Your grader isn't likely to mind if you do this; most graders are impressed by your attempt to organize things into a coherent whole. If you don't outline, you will get off the subject more easily, and, in the rush of writing, you may forget some important points.

Some answers may even be written in outline form. The fact that you are organized well enough to do that will usually impress your instructor. Don't make your outline skimpy, however, and don't use incomplete sentences. Number the main points and also the secondary ones. The primary reason that some instructors prefer essay exams over objective ones is that essay exams force you to organize information. You are much more likely to get credit for what you know if you express it in a well-organized form. Look at the two examples of brief answers to an essay question on pages 108–109 and see whether you can determine why one answer is better than the other.

Organizing Essay Answers

Here are two examples of brief answers to the same essay question. Read them to see what you think of them, and then compare your judgment with our comment below. The question is: "What were the important results of the (English) revolution of 1688?"

The first answer

I will summarize the most important results of the revolution under three headings:

1. *Parliament's victory.* The most direct result of the revolution of 1688 was the final victory of Parliament in the conflict between it and the crown that had gone on all during the 17th century. Parliament, by declaring the throne vacant because of James II's desertion to France, finally established that the king ruled by choice of the people and Parliament and not by divine right. Parliament established a Bill of Rights, which said that the king was not above the law but was himself subject to the law. In the early years of the reign of William and Mary, many additional acts were passed which curtailed the powers of the crown.

2. *The end of religious conflict.* The revolution itself did not entirely end the religious troubles of the 17th century, but Parliament passed a Toleration Act which brought an end to many of the difficulties of the Dissenters. The Catholics, however, were still subjected to many infringements of civil liberties.

3. *A new political class.* The important general result of the revolution and the victory of Parliament was the beginning of a long era during which political power in England was divided between the landed gentry and the merchant class.

Organizing Essay Answers (*Continued*)

The second answer

The revolution of 1688 was very important. It was so important that it is sometimes called the "glorious revolution." Parliament won, and it passed a lot of acts which were against the king, and it invited William and Mary to rule jointly in England. William and Mary still had to fight though, especially in Ireland where James II was finally defeated. William and Mary cooperated with Parliament so there wasn't so much trouble between the king and Parliament. James II was very unpopular because he was a Catholic, and Parliament made it so no Catholic could ever become king again, although parliament made things easier for the Dissenters. This was the end of the Divine Right of Kings in England, though at first the country was ruled mostly by the aristocracy and the rich merchants. Real democracy didn't come until much later, so the revolution of 1688 wasn't a completely democratic revolution.

Notice that these two answers differ more in organization than they do in content. The first answer is not perfect, but it is balanced, clear, and factual. The second is much poorer because it is vague, disorganized, and full of irrelevancies and loose statements.

Choosing Your Words

Be sure to choose your words carefully in answering an essay question. Instructors are not mind readers. They can't guess what you intended; they can only judge what you actually say. So say what you mean. Say it precisely. Give illustrations and examples if appropriate, and supply enough detail to make it clear that you know what you are talking about. The two examples on pages 108–109 of organized and disorganized answers illustrate the difference between precise, accurate statements and statements that, while they may be intended to say the same thing, don't say it in quite the right way. Know the difference between elaborating your points and padding your answer (also known as fudging). Bringing in extraneous points, repeating what you have already said, and being unnecessarily wordy are all padding. If you can't see the difference between the two examples in this respect, you may need some help in writing. Even though the poorly organized answer is shorter, it is full of padding. The other is not.

Writing Legibly and Correctly

Poor handwriting handicaps many students in essay exams. Instructors can't give you credit for something they can't read. Some instructors try hard to decipher illegible writing, but others have no patience with it and will mark down the illegible or barely legible paper. One study of the matter showed that an answer written in a poor hand was judged a point lower than the same answer written in a clear hand. And the readers in this study were told to ignore handwriting.

Take the trouble to put your answer is correct English. Punctuate properly and spell correctly. Poor writing implies disorganized and confused thinking as well as inadequate command of the subject matter. Poor spelling, especially of important or technical words, suggests careless reading and study. It is only natural that mistakes of this sort will pull your grade down.

TAKE-HOME EXAMS AND OPEN-BOOK EXAMS

Take-home and open-book exams are fairly common in college. They are most often to be found in courses in which there is an emphasis on problem solving—courses in such different subjects as mathematics, statistics, philosophy, and management. The purposes of these two types of tests are slightly different, and each requires a different approach.

Take-Home Exams

First of all, know the rules for take-home exams. Are you allowed to read the exam before you study for it? How much time are you given to complete the test? Usually you are allowed to use references but you are not allowed to discuss the exam with other students. The purpose of a take-home exam is not to emphasize factual information but rather your ability to solve problems. In a take-home statistics exam, for example, you may be given a set of data and asked to treat these data in the right way statistically. That will require you to understand the purpose of the data, to select the right statistical test to apply to the data, to apply that test to the data, and to interpret the result. In a philosophy exam, you may be asked to apply different sets of ethical principles to some life problems.

It is a mistake to put off studying until the take-home test is distributed. Part of your task is to decide what approach you should use to solve the given problem, and if you have not read the material, you may very well select the wrong method.

When you have decided what information you will need to solve the problem and have done the reading, plan your answer carefully. You might even outline the steps that you need to follow to answer the question. Then go about synthesizing information needed to answer the question. Work very carefully; minor mistakes might squeak by on a regular test but not on a take-home test. Whatever calculations you do must be double-checked; you will not get credit on the test if you have committed even the smallest error.

After you finish the exam, put it away for a little while. Then take it out and go over it again. Go through all the steps again. Be sure that you consider the alternatives. Make certain that you have made the right choice. Then review the reading and your notes, and, finally, recheck your calculations or reread your answer and make any changes that are necessary.

Open-Book Exams

Open-book exams are based on the same principle as take-home exams. They emphasize problem solving, thinking, and discovery. The primary difference is the limited time to complete open-book tests and they must be taken in the classroom. At best, you may have time to check certain points in the textbook or in your notes, look up formulas, consult tables, etc. You can't afford the time to review all the relevant material, so you must master the material beforehand. *You can't afford to study in the exam room.*

Check in your resources where it is necessary, but spend as much time as possible writing the exam. Plan your approach carefully. A logical organization counts for more in open-book exams than in ordinary exams. Make sure you have picked the correct technique or the right material with which to answer the question and then do the calculations or write your answer as legibly as you can. Show all the pertinent steps you used in the derivation of your answer if your exam is in mathematics, statistics, or the sciences.

Otherwise, all the hints for essay exams apply. Allocate your time among the questions, write legibly, and use correct English. Remember that you may have *less* time for each question because you will be expected to look up something or read a table or graph.

LEARNING FROM EXAMINATIONS

Exams are more than just a method used for assigning grades. At its essence an exam is another learning tool for you to use. To make the best use of an exam that has been returned to you, first make sure that the point value assigned to each problem has been calculated correctly. Sometimes mistakes are made. Don't hesitate to speak up if you find a mistake. Then be sure that you understand what you did wrong. Discuss (don't argue) any point for which you think that you were not graded fairly. It is far more important, however, to read your exam over and ask yourself, "Did I really understand what was asked for?"

If you study your exam carefully and get some feedback comments on it, you will achieve a deeper and better knowledge of the subject. You may uncover flaws in your study habits that you didn't notice before. You may find that there are gaps in your understanding despite your best efforts in studying. If that is the case, you may want to reassess your study plan. Mistakes, when promptly corrected, provide one of the best tools for learning.

Writing Papers

Can you put your ideas into words? The most important thing that most students get out of a college education is the ability to communicate at an intellectual level about difficult material. This means being able to read the material with understanding, to listen to and understand an intellectual presentation of the material, to be able to synthesize ideas, and then to present your ideas in oral or written form so that other educated people can understand them. This chapter is about writing in such diverse subjects as history, psychology, and marketing. The same steps are involved regardless of the subject; and the same writing techniques apply.

Most likely, you will be required to take a college-level course in English writing. Such a course can help you learn how to write accurately and clearly so that you can convey complicated ideas without getting hopelessly mixed up. In most of these courses you write themes or compositions, and the instructor goes over them carefully to tell you what you are doing right or wrong.

Many students hate to write. If you are one of them, the composition course will be a real chore and, unless you have a particularly good instructor, not very helpful. You may try to find easy topics and then write about them in a way so as to risk the least challenge by the instructor. Too bad. Even if you don't like your English writing course, you will face the challenge of writing in other courses. Good college instructors are sticklers about teaching you to write well. So if you are in a college that aims to really educate you, you are going to have to learn to write. We can't instruct you in writing—only someone who goes to the trouble of correcting what you write can do that—but we can provide you with some rules to make it easier for you to write well and to concentrate on learning how to write rather than just going through the motions.

Very few of you will become professional writers, but almost all of you will have jobs in which, from time to time, you will have to write clear, direct prose. Even if you only write letters to your mother, you will want to show that you can write well. We knew an engineer who was a supervisor for a whole office of engineers working on a very large project. He was so offended by the inability of his staff to write that he made them all attend a class in writing every Friday afternoon. Writing is *the* basic skill for educated people. No matter what you do after college, there will be times when you will have to write well enough to communicate something to other people.

We have written this chapter in such a way that it is mainly about writing term papers. We can't cover everything. You may find it useful to buy one of the many good handbooks of composition and manuals on writing that you can find in any college bookstore. These books go into greater depth than we do, and they are worth effort reading.

STEPS IN WRITING A PAPER

In this section we tell you about the steps to follow when writing a paper. Then we have a section on using the library and the Internet and taking research notes. In the final section we give you a little advice about the mechanics of writing.

Choosing a Topic

Sometimes your instructor will assign a topic for you to write on, but usually you will be given some freedom in picking your own topic. For English composition classes, you may be free to choose any topic that interests you.

Most instructors will warn you against picking a topic that is too broad or too difficult—the economy, religion, politics, computers, education, for example—but you will also have problems if you pick a topic that is too narrow or one in which you have a deep personal involvement. You may flounder around because you just "can't think of anything to say."

One way to find topics for a particular course is to scan through the indexes of textbooks and scholarly books on the subject. Suppose, for example, you are taking a course on American political history. You may find an entry in your textbook index, "Conventions, beginnings of." You turn to the pages indicated and find three or four paragraphs on the subject. You read that, at first, presidential candidates were nominated in secret by caucuses of congressional representatives, but by the 1830s this system was replaced by open nominating conventions. How this came about might interest you, and so you tentatively pick the topic: "The rise of nominating conventions." By way of practice, pick up a textbook and see how many topics you can identify that might be suitable for a term paper.

Lecture notes are another source of topics. Make special note of things that come up in lectures that might interest you. Look for topics that relate to your major. If you have a major in speech pathology and are taking a course in the psychology of language, you might find the instructor alluding to the problems of language development of the deaf. That could provide a topic for you.

For some kinds of papers you may have to look for other ways to find topics. In one engineering course, for example, students are required to do a project on the design of common household articles. The student must select something such as a stove, a vacuum cleaner, or even a broom and tell what is wrong with its design and how to improve it. Here the trick is to pick something that allows you to show some ingenuity and originality.

Many of your instructors will ask for papers based on your daily experiences. Most of us write best about things we are involved in and are interested in. If you are taking a sociology course and studying social organization, for example, you might want to write a paper about the role of the hometown high school basketball team in the social structure of the town.

Other good topics come from the relationship between different courses you are taking. You may be taking a course in U.S. history and one in twentieth-century American literature. For the literature course, you may have read and liked one of the novels by Sinclair Lewis. For the history course, then, you could write a paper on the social changes of the 1920s depicted in three Lewis novels—*Main Street, Babbitt,* and *Elmer Gantry.*

Choosing a topic that is likely to interest the instructor is, by the way, a good rule. This isn't as crass as it sounds. Good writers always take into account their potential audience, and your main audience for a term paper is your instructor. If you don't know what the instructor is interested in, choose an important topic, one that would likely interest a number of people.

But even more important is choosing a topic that interests you. To do a good job, you will have to spend a fair amount of time working on the topic, so it should be something that you want to learn more about or some idea or experience that you want to understand better.

Gathering Data

How you gather material for your paper depends on your topic, the type of paper required, and its length and complexity. Sometimes you will have to do very little reading and instead write an informal essay on something of personal interest. More often, however, you will probably have to make extensive use of the library, the Internet, and other research methods such as interviews and statistical experiments. And you will have to take research notes.

To get started, you should do some background reading. Your textbook or other books you have read in the course usually can supply some background. If you get stuck, your instructor can help you clarify or limit your topic and perhaps supply some sources for background reading. In many cases, these background sources will furnish a bibliography that will lead you to other materials. In other cases, you will have to go to abstracts, cumulative indexes, or special bibliographic sources to compile a list of things you should read. And, of course, once you have begun to read in earnest, you will find additional references.

As you consult your references, you will prepare a working bibliography. Unless you're a real computer jockey with access to some good indexing programs, you'll keep your working bibliography on 3- by 5-inch or 4- by 6-inch cards. Later, if you wish, you may transfer from file card notes to a computer disk, but the cards are best. We discuss later the various computer programs for retrieving books from a catalog. Your library probably has one of these programs, and you may use a cut-and-paste approach to making out cards for books. Generally, though, this won't work for periodicals, so you will inevitably have to make some handwritten notes. Let's assume you will use cards.

For each book or article you consult, prepare a card that contains the following information: (1) the author(s) of the book or article (also any editor or translator); (2) the title and edition of the book, and, if available, the library call number. If you use the library's card catalog or printout program, all that information will come automatically, but if you work directly from the book, make sure that you get the information about the name of the book and the author from the title page, not from the spine. For books you will need (3) place of publication; (4) name of publisher; (5) copyright date. Most of the time you will find this information on the back of the title page. For articles you will need (6) the volume number of the journal or magazine, if given; (7) the year the magazine was issued; (8) the page numbers of the article if the journal or magazine cumulates page numbers throughout the year; if the page numbers are for just a single issue, you will need to note the month or date of issue as well as the page numbers.

Assign a number (1, 2, 3, . . .) to each bibliography card and write it in the upper right-hand corner.

As you read, take notes either on the back of the cards or on separate cards, and code the cards to correspond to the bibliography card. Study the sample bibliography cards on pages 118 and 119. If you are careful and accurate in preparing your cards, you will save yourself time and grief when you are ready to compile your final bibliography.

Notes for a paper that is based on library research are not like the notes you take from textbooks. Research notes are usually not outlines. Instead they are in the form of summaries or quotes. *Make sure you indicate very clearly when you are quoting.* Even famous scholars have been called to task for using other people's words without attribution. Not indicating direct quotations can mean deep trouble for students, and, in some institutions with strong honor codes, it can mean expulsion. A safe way to make sure you get a quote right is to photocopy the relevant pages from the source.

How long or detailed your summary is depends on the length of the reading, on what the instructor has suggested you do, and your purpose in reading. You can make rough reading notes as you go along, but after you have made a summary of them you can discard your rough notes. Once again, be sure to distinguish between summaries and quotes from the author. If you quote, be sure to note the page number of the quote.

Another thing about taking notes for a research paper is that you don't know exactly how many notes you will use for your paper until you have finished reading all your material. Your original topic may turn out to be too big, or some of the sources you read may prove to be irrelevant or unimportant. Nor do you know as you read just how you will organize your paper. It is a sure thing that you will not organize your paper in the order that your notes were taken. That is why it is useful to take notes on cards. For a large paper requiring lots of cards, you will need a card box in which to file them. If you buy a thousand cards at a time (not as expensive as it sounds), you will prob-

Bibliography Cards

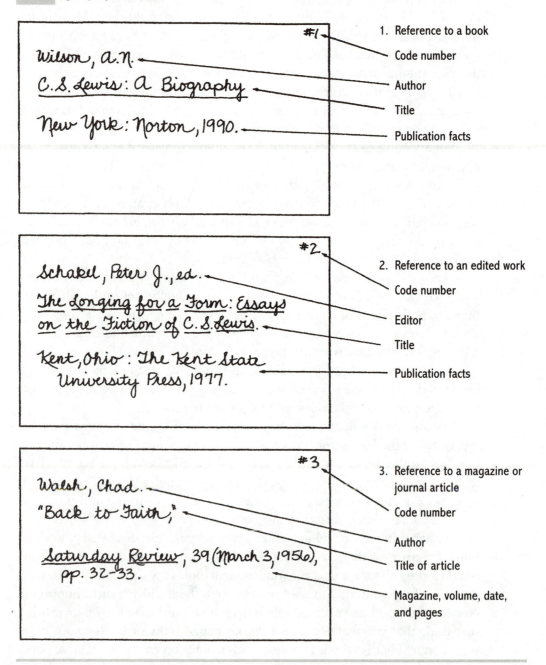

#1

Wilson, A. N.
C. S. Lewis: A Biography
New York: Norton, 1990.

1. Reference to a book
   Code number
   Author
   Title
   Publication facts

#2

Schakel, Peter J., ed.
The Longing for a Form: Essays on the Fiction of C. S. Lewis.
Kent, Ohio: The Kent State University Press, 1977.

2. Reference to an edited work
   Code number
   Editor
   Title
   Publication facts

#3

Walsh, Chad.
"Back to Faith,"
Saturday Review, 39 (March 3, 1956), pp. 32-33.

3. Reference to a magazine or journal article
   Code number
   Author
   Title of article
   Magazine, volume, date, and pages

Note Card, Corresponding Bibliography Card, and Quote Card

Study the sample note card and its corresponding bibliography card.

(#1)

Influence of Charles Williams on C. S. Lewis.
Williams was a great friend of Lewis and given a warm welcome when he arrived in Oxford. He became a regular member of the Inklings. Though Lewis denied being consciously influenced by Williams in his work, Green believes that the unconscious influence of Williams made the war years productive for Lewis.
p. 184

— Code number
— Topic heading

— Note
— Page reference

(#1)

Green, Roger L., and Hooper, Walter.
C. S. Lewis - A Biography
New York & London: Harcourt, Brace Jovanovich (Harvest Books), 1974.

The code number on both the note card and the bibliography card tells you the source of the note.

Suppose you had decided not to code your references. Another note card in this example would then be in the following form:

Green & Hooper
C.S. Lewis-A Biography
Lewis - Early Childhood
"I am a product of long corridors, empty sunlit rooms, upstair indoor silences, attics explored in solitude ..."
Written by Lewis in his autobiography
p. 20

— Abbreviated version of author and title
— Topic heading
— Note (a direct quotation)
— Use of ellipsis, indicating that part of a sentence is missing
— Page

ably get a sturdy box with them. Otherwise you can buy a metal or plastic box at your college bookstore. You should also buy alphabetic dividers. People who do a lot of writing of factual books and articles almost always do this.

You should index your cards by topics. If, for example, you are summarizing an article about smoking and heart disease, the topic heading on your card might be "Smoking—effects of nicotine on heart rate." Most summaries will fit on one card, but if you do need more than one, label the cards a, b, c, . . . Make sure that you code each card with its source.

When you copy an author directly, make sure you copy accurately. If you use only part of a direct quotation, use an ellipsis (three dots) to show that you have left something out (on purpose).

All this may seem complicated and cumbersome at first, but once you are used to the card system for taking research notes, you will find it easy. If you use a computer to store your research notes, be sure that the information is arranged in such a way that you can not only easily retrieve it but also print out a bibliography quickly and easily.

Constructing an Outline

About the time you are finished taking notes, you will want to begin to think about the form of your paper. Making an outline is not a bad idea. First read through your note cards and arrange them according to the topic headings that are forming in your mind. This will give you some idea about how your paper should be organized. If you construct an outline, arrange the main and subordinate headings in a good, logical order. If you haven't read what we have to say about the format of outlines (pages 84–89), read it now before you begin.

It depends on how you work best, but for most people spending a few extra minutes on an outline is worth it. It will make your paper better organized and your writing job an easier one. After you begin writing, you may want to revise your outline or just use it as a guide and a reminder as to what needs to be said. An outline may also tell you that you have to do some more reading or that you may have to make a small section into a more substantial one.

Writing the First Draft

Very few people can get by with just one draft. There are a few famous authors who can pull it off, but most careful writers go through several drafts. Two drafts should do for most term papers, but something as important as a senior thesis may require more.

If you've made an outline, rearrange your notes to follow the order of your outline. Then write. For writing, allow yourself a large block of time during which you can work without interruptions. Writing a long paper in one session is a big undertaking, but many students can do it, particularly if the paper is fewer than ten pages. For a first draft, don't worry too much about getting everything exactly right. Some writers just leave a space when they know they can come back later and fill in something that is not essential to the organization of the paper. Once you get your essential ideas down, you can correct things easily enough.

Leave plenty of room for corrections and alterations. *Never, never* single-space a first draft, even if the final version is going to be single-spaced. You will certainly be using a computer with a word processor, and you can single space the first draft if you want to and double-space the first printout, even if you have made the corrections on the screen. When you have completed the first draft, go over it for obvious changes. No one is going to see your first draft but you (unless your instructor asks to see it).

If possible, allow as much time as possible between the first draft and a revision. This will give you a fresh perspective, and it will be easier for you to detect mistakes and lapses in grammar and writing.

Revising the Paper

After you have put your work aside for a while, it's time to revise. First *check that you included everything that should be included.* Is there anything that slipped by in the first draft? Did you not explain certain topics sufficiently? You may need to go back to your notes for something you left out or for something you may not have gotten quite right. You may even have to go back to the library to check on something or to dig up additional material. If you want to produce a really good paper, it is worth the effort.

Then check the organization of your paper. Does it hang together? Be critical of yourself because your instructor certainly will be. Are headings and subheadings in the right places and clearly indicated with their relative weight. Are the transitions between sections smooth? Should you have a summary and a conclusion? If you are not satisfied with your organization, change it. It may mean simply a cut-and-paste job or moving paragraphs on the computer. Or it may mean rewriting sentences and even whole paragraphs.

Finally, check the mechanics. Are your sentences grammatical and understandable? Do you have some wordy and awkward constructions? (Your word processor will help you with this.) Look at your verbs. Do you overuse all-purpose but sometimes meaningless verbs such as "involve"? Do you use the passive voice monotonously? If you don't know what the passive voice is, stop now and look it up. You will, of course, have a good dictionary handy, but, in addition, refresh your understanding of what is good style by reviewing a concise handbook such as Strunk and White's *The Elements of Style*. We have more to say about this later.

Documenting Your Paper

When you write a paper using other people's ideas, you must give credit to your sources. Using someone else's ideas or the discoveries reported by other people without acknowledging your debt is described by a single word—plagiarism. Plagiarism is a serious offense. As we mention before, in many colleges plagiarism is grounds for dismissal.

In a research paper, documentation may be given in the text with footnotes that are keyed to a bibliography. The footnote may give the full reference, the author and title, or merely the author and date. If the reference is well known and short, you can acknowledge it in the text (not as a footnote) and not enter the source in the bibliography. A biblical reference is an example. "When I was a child, I spoke as a child. . . ." (I Corinthians 13:11) (Exception: If you use a new or not well-known translation of the Bible, you should refer to it by footnote.) Other references that do not need footnotes include well-known quotes from literature: "Good night, sweet prince, and flights of angels sing they to thy rest." (Hamlet, v. ii 59) Well-known sayings do not need to be footnoted. You might write: As Harry Truman said, "If you can't stand the heat, get out of the kitchen."

Footnotes belong either at the bottom of the page, numbered consecutively, or in a list at the end of the paper (technically, in this case they are called endnotes). The number of the footnote appears as a superscript in the appropriate place in the text. Sources that you use merely for background material and that you do not directly draw upon can simply be cited in your bibliography. The endnotes do not constitute a bibliography. You must have a complete listing of your source material.

There are several ways to do footnoting. Consult a style manual such as *The MLA Style Sheet* published by the Modern Languages Association. There are dozens of others. Some instructors have a preference for a particular style. If so, find out what it is and *follow it*. Most of these sources give you forms of citation and keys to standard abbreviations (op. cit., ibid., etc.). Whatever form you choose, be consistent in your use.

In the social sciences and to a degree in the natural sciences, each discipline has its own form for citation. For example, in a psychology course you might say in a paper: "It is well known that autonomic responses may be influenced by cognitive activity. (Jones, 1988)" If there are two or more references in the same year by the same author, add letters to the year: "(Jones, 1988a; Jones, 1988b)." Be sure to find out whether or not your instructor wants you to use this form. But also be sure *not* to use it where it would be inappropriate. If you are a psychology major, this form probably comes naturally, but don't spring it on your English instructor.

There is an art to knowing what information needs to be acknowledged by a citation and what information is general knowledge. If you are going to err, err on the side of too much documentation rather than too little. When in doubt, acknowledge your source.

Your final bibliography will consist of all the works you consulted in the research for your paper even if you do not refer to a work directly in a footnote. Since you already have your working bibliography on cards or on a disk, all you need to do is go through the cards and eliminate the references that you did not use and prepare a list alphabetized according to the authors' last names. (In footnotes, authors' names come first.) If you cite more than one work by the same author, list these in alphabetical order by title. Caution: In some disciplines you are expected to list multiple works by the same author according to date. Also, in the social and natural sciences you usually do not list works that you have read but have not actually cited. We include a sample bibliography on page 125.

Preparing the Final Draft

By this time you will probably feel that your job is finished and that you will want to get the final version printed as soon as possible. But if you can, set the paper aside for a day or two. You will likely want to make a few more corrections before you print the final version. This is particularly true if it is a major paper. We realize that students frequently stay up all night working on a paper that is due the next day, but if the paper is important to you or if your entire grade rests on it, our advice is to plan ahead enough so that you have time to give it a rest for a day or so before you turn it in.

A term paper should never be presented in handwritten form. If you don't have a computer and don't know how to type, you should hire someone to enter it in a word processor and print it out. Most instructors will not even accept it in handwritten form. Use a good grade of paper (not the erasable kind), standard size, and print *double-spaced*. Never turn in a paper that is

Page with Footnotes

The following is a page from a term paper on Margaret Fuller, a nineteenth-century feminist. This excerpt illustrates the use and form of footnotes in term papers.

> In Mount Auburn cemetery in Cambridge, Massachusetts, is a memorial stone raised following the death by shipwreck in 1850 of Margaret Fuller, Marchesa Ossoli. The inscription on this stone reads in part: "By birth a child of New England, By adoption a citizen of Rome. . . . In youth . . . seeking the highest culture   In maturer years, earnest reformer in America and Europe."[1]
>
> If a few words carved on a gravestone can sum up the span of a life, these words do so for Sarah Margaret Fuller. This paper explores briefly her passage from the rarefied culture of New England Transcendentalism to the European revolutionary movement of 1848. For, although Margaret Fuller was formed by the New England of the early nineteenth century and molded in its image, she left the peace of Concord, the familiar intellectual world of Cambridge, for the bustle of New York, and then, beckoned by her long cherished dream of Italy, she arrived finally in Rome where she found her spiritual home.[2] From a youth devoted to culture of self, she moved to reform and finally to participation in the Roman revolution of 1848.
>
> The young Margaret's worship of genius and power and her disdain for the "vulger herd"[3] became the faith of the mature woman in the unspoiled nature of the people.[4] Her early desire to remain aloof from such experiments in . . . .

1. Mason Wade, *Margaret Fuller: Whetstone of Genius,* Viking, New York, 1940, pp. 271–272.
2. R. W. Emerson et al., *Memoirs of Margaret Fuller Ossoli,* v. 2, Phillips, Samuels & Co., Boston, 1852, p. 216.
3. Ibid., v. 1, p. 134.
4. Ibid., v. 2, p. 225.

single-spaced unless you are specifically required to do that. If you place your footnotes at the bottom of the page, they can be single-spaced and set off from the text by a line extending across the paper. You will find a sample with this form of citation above. Number every page except the title page in the upper right-hand corner.

Sample Bibliography

Here is a sample bibliography for a term paper on "Gender in Contemporary Higher Education."

Archer, J., and Lloyd, B. B. (1985). *Sex and gender.* Cambridge: Cambridge University Press.

Astin, A. W. (1977). *Four critical years.* San Francisco: Jossey-Bass.

Astin, A. W., Green, K. C., Korn, W. S., and Schalit, M. (1986). *The American freshman: National norms for fall 1986.* Los Angeles: Cooperative Institutional Research Program, Graduate School of Education, University of California.

Bernard, J. (1972) *The sex game.* New York: Atheneum.

Chickering, A. W. et al. (eds.) (1981). *The modern American college.* San Francisco: Jossey-Bass.

El-Khawas, E. H. (1988). *Community college fact book.* New York: Macmillan.

Gerson, J. M. Women returning to school: The consequences of multiple roles. *Sex roles, 13,* 1–2, 77–92.

Harding, S. G. (1986). *The science question in feminism.* Ithaca, New York: Cornell University Press.

Henley, N., and Barrie, T. (eds.) (1975). *Language and sex: Difference and dominance.* Rowley, Massachusetts: Newbury House.

Mendelsohn, P. (1986). *Happier by degrees.* Berkeley, California: Ten Speed Press.

Springer, M. (1988). Women and power in higher education: Saving the Libra in a Scorpio world. In S. S. Brehm (ed.), *Seeing female: social roles and personal lives* (pp. 145–156). New York: Greenwood Press.

When the paper has been printed or copied in its final form, proofread it carefully. We all make mistakes. *Make sure you have a duplicate copy before you turn the paper in.*

USING THE LIBRARY

The library is the heart of every college or university. If you don't use the library, you are missing the most important intellectual treat your college has to offer. You go there to gather material for the papers you write, to find the required and supplemental readings for your classes, to study when your dormitory or home is too noisy, and, yes, just to enjoy the best works that civilization has to offer. You may not know all the things that the library, even a small library, can do for you. If you are in a big school, don't let the size of the library intimidate you. Libraries are organized on logical principles, and librarians are there to help you.

Layout of the Library

Learn how your library is organized. Big institutions usually have several libraries. In fact, in the biggest colleges, individual departments have their own libraries. In most research universities there will be both an undergraduate library and a research library. In some institutions the research library is open to everyone—if it is, browse in it. In others, you need special status—usually being a faculty member or graduate student—to use it. Don't let that discourage you. Even if you can't enter the stacks, you can check materials out. In rare book collections you may have to have someone photocopy material in order to use it. Persist; you can always get access to what you need if you try hard enough.

You may now browse some libraries electronically, and they are linked throughout the world. It is possible to sit at your computer at home and find listings for libraries across the country. With cooperative agreements among libraries, you can check out material from virtually anywhere it can be found.

During orientation or as soon as possible after you arrive on campus, go to the library and look around. At most colleges, the library staff will present orientation tours of the library. By all means go to one. Larger libraries have directories posted at various points to guide you. Some libraries publish manuals that list and describe the services they offer. In any event, take advantage of whatever your library offers by way of introduction to library services. It is absolutely essential that you know where to find the following:

1. Card catalogs and computerized retrieval systems. The card catalog tells you what is in the library, and via a coding system (in most institutions the Library of Congress system), how to find what you want. In the traditional card catalog there are usually cards in three categories—author, title, and subject. These types of cards are illustrated on page 127.

In bigger libraries card catalogs are being phased out in favor of electronic retrieval programs. These differ slightly from institution to institution (they

Catalog Cards by Subject, Author, and Title

Subject

```
            MOGUL EMPIRE—HISTORY
DS
461    Hansen, Waldemar.
H33        The Peacock Throne : the drama of
1981   Mogul India / Waldemar Hansen.—Delhi
       :  Motilal Banarsidass, 1981.
          xi, 560 p. : ill. ; 25 cm.
          Bibliography: p. 533–545.
          First Indian reprint of the 1972 edition.
          Includes index.

          1. Mogul Empire—History.    2. India—History—1500–1765.
       3. Taj Mahal—History.    4. Shahjahan, Emperor of India,
       ca. 1592–1666.    I. Title.
```

Author

```
       Gilder, George F., 1939–
HB             Wealth and poverty / George Gilder.—New York : Basic
501    Books, c1981.
.G46
               xii, 306 p. ; 24 cm.

               Bibliography: p. 289–295.
               Includes index.
               ISBN 0-465-09105-9 : $16.95

               1. Capitalism.   2. Wealth.   3. United States—Economic
       conditions—1945–.    4. United States—Economic policy.   I. Title
       HB501.G46              330.12′2—dc19           80-50556

       Library of Congress
```

Title

```
       Computers in video production
PN
1992   McQuillin, Lon B.
.75        Computers in video production / by Lon McQuillin.—White
M36    Plains, NY : Knowledge Industry Publications, c1986.

           x, 186 p. : ill. ; 29 cm.—(video bookshelf)

           Bibliography: p. 167–170.
           Includes index.
           ISBN 0-86729-182-6 : $39.95

           1. Television—Production and direction—Data processing.
       I. Title. II. Series
       PN1992.75.M36          1986

       Library of Congress
```

even have different names: At the University of Virginia it is called Virgo; at Georgetown University it is called George). These systems are user-friendly, but even so, you should learn how to use them as soon as possible. Most of them provide printouts of what you call for (see samples of retrieval printouts on page 129), and you can use these printouts as your sources (remember that you can make your bibliography cards by cutting-and-pasting from these printouts).

2. Reading rooms. Larger libraries usually have several reading rooms, one for each of several functions or subjects. For example, there may be a reference reading room and one for periodicals. Smaller libraries may have one general reading room. Check them out. In some of the newer libraries, often called learning or media centers, there may be no specific reading rooms, but, instead, comfortable chairs and tables scattered throughout the stacks or wherever the books are located.

3. Computer facilities. Modern campuses abound with computer facilities, but the ones intended for the typical undergraduate student usually will be found in the library. Find out about these and go to whatever orientation session is offered that explains how to use them. Many of these facilities are open around the clock (we've heard students say that their paper was late or poorly edited because they couldn't get on a computer until 3 a.m.). Find out where all of your computer facilities are located, and your library is bound to be one of them.

4. Reference facilities. Reference works are kept separate from the general books and periodicals. They are sometimes kept in a separate reference room. These rooms include encyclopedias, biographical dictionaries, yearbooks, and other valuable resources. These reference works cannot be taken from the library, but you can usually photocopy anything you want. Something students don't know is that there is always a librarian who specializes in reference. If you are in despair because you don't know where to look in the reference section, consult the reference librarian.

5. Current periodicals. Current periodicals are usually shelved in a periodical room or in a separate section at the back of the main reading room. Back issues are bound and shelved along with books by subject matter. Occasionally, however, they are shelved separately, particularly in smaller departmental or branch libraries. If you need a periodical from the last year or two and can't find it on the shelves, ask the librarian about it. It may be out being

Sample Retrieval Printout

```
VCAT SEARCH REQUEST: A=DEESE JAMES
BIBLIOGRAPHIC RECORD -- NO. 6 OF 16 ENTRIES FOUND

Morgan, Clifford Thomas.
   How to study : Morgan and Deese's classic handbook for students. --
3d ed.  rev. / by James Deese, Ellin K. Deese. -- New York :
McGraw-Hill, 1979.
   vi, 118 p. : ill. ; 26 cm. -- (McGraw-Hill paperbacks)
   Includes index.
  SUBJECT HEADINGS (Library of Congress; use s= ):
    Study, Method of.


LOCATION: EDUCATION LIBRARY
CALL NUMBER: LB1049 .M68 1979
    Not charged out.




TYPE n FOR NEXT RECORD. TYPE i FOR INDEX.
TYPE r TO REVISE SEARCH, h FOR HELP, e FOR INTRO TO VCAT.
TYPE COMMAND AND PRESS ENTER==>




  VCAT SEARCH REQUEST: K=SHAKESPEARE AND MIDSUMMER
  BIBLIOGRAPHIC RECORD -- NO. 13 OF 143 ENTRIES FOUND

Lynch, Ina Celeste.
  The creation of the role of Helena in A midsummer night's dream / Ina
Celeste Lynch. -- 1985.
   36 leaves, [1],[8] leaves of plates : ill. (some mounted, some col.)
 ; 29 cm. Thesis (M.F.A.)--University of Virginia, 1985.
  Bibliography: leaf [37].
 SUBJECT HEADINGS (Library of Congress; use s= ):
   Shakespeare, William, 1564-1616. Midsummer night's dream.
   Shakespeare, William, 1564-1616--Characters--Helena.
   Acting-Study and teaching--Virginia.


LOCATION: FINE ARTS Theses
CALL NUMBER: Masters Drama 1985 .L96
    Not charged out.



      FOR ANOTHER COPY AT THIS OR ANOTHER LOCATION, press ENTER

TYPE n FOR NEXT RECORD. TYPE i FOR INDEX.
TYPE r TO REVISE SEARCH, h FOR HELP, e FOR INTRO TO VCAT.
TYPE COMMAND AND PRESS ENTER==>
```

bound, or it may be missing. In any event you will be doing a service by asking about it. Periodicals from more than 1 or 2 years ago are usually available on microfilm or microfiche. Be sure that you know how to use microfilm and microfiche equipment.

6. Stacks. "Stacks" is a word for a series of shelves on which the books are arranged for compact storage. The shelves are spaced just far enough apart to let you get between them. The stacks in big universities may cover several floors of a large building. Stacks are even *open* or *closed*. Open stacks are available to all users of the library. They are usually found in smaller, undergraduate institutions, though some of the largest and best research universities pride themselves on maintaining open stacks for everybody. Closed stacks require a special permit for entry. They are usually restricted to faculty and graduate students. If your library has open stacks, you may go directly to the shelves to find the books you want (and better yet, you can freely browse through the stacks). If it has closed stacks, then you need to fill out a request card and wait for the library staff to get your book for you. If you can't find what you want in the undergraduate library, *do not hesitate to go to the research library.* As we pointed out earlier, even if you aren't given free access, you can probably get what you want through persistence.

7. Reserve shelves. Every college library has a separate section of reserve shelves. In this section the books are shelved according to *courses* in which they are used. They are identified by course number or instructor's name. The idea behind reserve shelves is to be sure that everyone in a class has access to the required and supplemental reading. These books sometimes do not circulate; they can be used only in the library. If they do circulate, it is usually for a short time, perhaps overnight. Penalties for late return of reserve materials is steep, so make sure that you return them on time.

8. Special collections and facilities. Most libraries, even those with open stacks, have some material, often valuable or rare books and manuscripts, kept in special rooms. For protection, these materials may only be viewed on microfilm or microfiche. Most libraries have record and tape collections for foreign languages, music, poetry, and drama. More and more have videotapes, CDs, and DVDs for circulation.

If a book you need is not in your library, it can usually be obtained for you on loan from another library. Check with a librarian before you decide that it isn't available.

Most large libraries provide daily computer printouts that list all books currently checked out. If the book you want is not on the shelf, check the printout and ask the librarian to request that it be returned. If the book is neither on the shelf nor circulating, have the librarian put out a search for it.

Classification

Everything in the library is classified according to one of two systems: The Dewey decimal system has been almost replaced by the Library of Congress system. The Library of Congress system uses letters of the alphabet for its general subject divisions and numerals for finer distinctions. Within each subject class a letter stands for the author's name, followed by a serial number to distinguish among books in this category. For example, *Wealth and Poverty* by George Gilder has the number HB501.G46. HB is the code for economics (H by itself stands for social sciences generally); the number 501 stands for a particular subject matter in economics. The G46 is the specific number for the book (G is the first letter of the author's last name). This letter and numeral combination constitutes the call number or location symbol for the book. It tells you or the library clerk where to find the book.

You can't rely on any classification system to lead you infallibly to the right books. Classification is always a matter of judgment, and there are always gray areas. You may want something that falls between linguistics and anthropology or between psychology and biology, so watch for topics you want and not the classification numbers.

Card Catalogs and Computer Retrieval Systems

As noted before, books are classified three ways: by *author,* by *title,* and by *subject.* Some libraries file all cards in a single alphabetical arrangement, but others, particularly big libraries, use a *divided catalog system.* In these systems, one card catalog contains cards alphabetized by author and title, while the other contains the subject cards. All computerized systems have all three types accessible in the system.

The subject catalog, whether in a computerized retrieval system or in a traditional card catalog, is particularly useful in the early stages of doing a research paper. You can look up a topic and thumb through the cards or scan the computer screen for items that appear to be unusual or interesting. Later, when you know what author or title you are after, you can use the author and title entries to locate particular books. In some computerized systems the subject listing goes by the name "key word."

Here are some rules you should know in order to use the catalog efficiently:

1. Cards and entries are alphabetized according to the first word of the entry. This will vary depending on whether this word is the author, title, or subject. In book titles, words such as *the, a,* or *an* are neglected. *The Politics of Jacksonian Finance* by John M. McFaul would be filed under the Ps by title, under the Ms by author, and under the Us by subject (United States–Politics and Government 1815–1861).

2. Headings containing abbreviations such as St. and Mt. are alphabetized as if they were spelled out in full. Names beginning with Mc or Mac are alphabetized as if they were all spelled Mac. Thus:
MacAdams, Alta.
McAdams, David.
McGuire, J.
Machado, A.

3. Most libraries alphabetize titles and subjects consisting of more than one word in a word-by-word filing system. Thus the order would be New York, Newark. Some libraries, however, use a letter-by-letter system without regard to spacing between words; here Newark would come first and New York second.

4. The titles of books that begin with numbers are alphabetized as if the numbers were spelled out. For example, *20,000 Leagues Under the Sea* would be filed under the Ts.

5. Subdivisions of historical subjects are usually arranged chronologically, as in the following:
United States–Politics and Government
1783–1814.
United States–Politics and Government
1815–1861.

6. Subdivisions of other subjects are usually alphabetical, as in the following:
France–Art.
France–Geography.
France–Government.
France–Music.

7. People are listed before places, places before subjects, and subjects before titles, as in the following two listings:

Jefferson, Thomas.

Jefferson City, Missouri.

Jefferson, by A. J. Nock.

Mineral, Virginia.

Mineral.

Mineral Deposits, by W. Lindgren.

8. Books *by* a person are listed before books *about* a person, as in:

Sinclair, Upton, *World's End.*

Sinclair, Upton, *Upton Sinclair, American Rebel,* by Leon Harris.

Periodical Indexes

Much of your research for writing papers will be in periodicals, especially for more advanced courses. You will want to consult *The Readers' Guide to Periodical Literature,* the most useful index of its kind. It lists articles appearing in popular magazines and less technical journals. For more advanced research, particularly in the humanities, arts, and social sciences, the *International Index of Periodicals* is the source to use. But almost every discipline has its own abstract or index publication. One of the more helpful things you can do when you choose your major is to find out what the basic abstract or index system is in your discipline.

Abstracts

Abstracts go beyond merely indexing the literature in a particular field; they summarize the articles so that readers can determine which ones will be useful. Whenever abstracts are available, consult them. They can be of great help in putting together a bibliography. The best-known examples of abstracts are *Chemical Abstracts, Biological Abstracts, Psychological Abstracts,* and *Educational Abstracts.* These all put out indexes at annual or semiannual intervals. So, to find articles in these fields, go to the index for the year (if the abstracts are not yet bound for that year, they will be in a separate issue), jot down the abstract number, and scan the abstract to see if the article will be helpful. If it looks promising, write down the whole entry, look up the journal in the catalog to find its call number, and then request the journal so that you can read the original article.

Newspaper Indexes

If you need current newspaper articles, your best bet is *The New York Times Index,* which covers all the important articles published in that newspaper. Despite its name, *The New York Times* is the closest thing we have to a national newspaper or newspaper of record in the United States. Nearly every college library subscribes to the paper itself, to its *Index,* and usually to the microfilm edition. Even if you intend to go to other newspapers, *The New York Times* is the place to start. The *Index* dates events precisely enough for you to look them up in other newspapers or magazines.

Reference Books

Reference books are useful not only for digging out materials for research papers but also for answering questions that may interest you. There are a lot of them: encyclopedias, dictionaries, yearbooks, atlases, gazetteers, books of quotations, and many more.

Encyclopedias   If you want to look up a particular topic such as mathematics in ancient Greece, a general encyclopedia is the best place to start. The most commonly used encyclopedia in America, despite its name is *Encyclopaedia Britannica,* but for many purposes there are others, including *Encyclopedia Americana,* that are as good or better. If your library is a large one, it will contain many encyclopedias, including such specialized works as the *McGraw-Hill Encyclopedia of Science and Technology* and the *International Encyclopedia of the Social Sciences.* There are others in such fields as music and art. *Grove's Dictionary of Music and Musicians,* despite its title, is really an encyclopedia about music.

Yearbooks (Annuals)   To find out what happened in a particular year, consult one of the yearbooks. *The American Annual* (*1923–*) is the annual supplement to the *Encyclopedia Americana,* and the *Britannica Book of the Year* (*1938–*) is a similar supplement to the *Encyclopaedia Britannica.* Both contain articles covering events or important developments in the year named.

Other yearbooks and almanacs contain statistical information, miscellaneous facts, and brief summaries of events. They give you almost any conceivable kind of statistical fact. Among these publications are the following:

The World Almanac and Book of Facts (*1868–*) is a stupendous compendium of facts, mostly about the United States. Here you can find everything from the population of some remote hamlet in Kansas to the birth dates of movie stars.

Information Please Almanac (*1947–*) is a similar compendium with fewer statistics and more articles.

Whitaker's Almanack (*1869–*) is a British publication similar to the *World Almanac.*

The Statesman's Yearbook (*1864–*) contains information about world governments.

Statistical Abstract of the United States (*1878–*) is a government publication containing statistical information about industrial, social, political, and economic aspects of the United States.

Dictionaries   A dictionary, as we usually think about it, is a book of words, alphabetically arranged, that you consult to find proper spellings, meanings, usages, and derivations. There are dictionaries of languages (French-English, English-Spanish, etc.) and biographical dictionaries. You will also find specialized dictionaries that deal with topics such as medicine, biology, or physics.

Libraries have unabridged dictionaries of the English language that are usually too large and expensive for home. Among them is *Webster's Third New International Dictionary* published by Merriam-Webster Company; *Funk and Wagnalls New Standard Dictionary,* and the biggest of them all, the *Oxford English Dictionary,* the OED. In most cases these are sources to consult when you need to know about the history of words or about some unusual, perhaps obsolete, usage of a familiar word.

If you are bogged down in technical lingo of some specialized subject, such as chemistry, psychology, medicine, or biology, you can consult dictionaries restricted to these disciplines. While few of you will want to own one or more of these expensive books, make use of them in the library (there's another good reason for studying in the library).

When you want information about people, use a biographical dictionary. For Americans no longer living who were influential during their lifetime, there is the *Dictionary of American Biography.* For important people in Great Britain, there is a reference series called the *Dictionary of National Biography.* For people who are still living, there are various *Who's Who* volumes. *Who's Who* itself contains information mainly about people in Great Britain. *Who's Who in America* is the most general biographical reference work for living Americans. But there are many such publications. The trick is to find the right one. The

U.S. government through the Government Printing Office (the GPO) issues valuable pamphlets and official publications. There are clipping services to which your library might subscribe for items of local interest. And there are audiovisual materials of various types available for your use in your library.

Reference Librarians

Most libraries have librarians whose chief function is to help with references. Faculty members consult them all the time, but they really like to help students. If you are in doubt about where to look up something, go to the reference desk. People there can help.

In General

The number of books and articles published each year is almost beyond comprehension. Nevertheless, by using reference books, abstracts, indexes, and the like, you can track down one particular fact about the most obscure topic imaginable from the whole mass of material the library contains. The ability to use these resources puts the whole world of printed and computer-based information at your disposal. It is one of the best things a college education can give you. The future belongs to the information explosion, and if you are going to be there to grasp what belongs to you, there is no better place to start than in college and in the college library.

IMPROVING WRITING SKILLS

The ability to write well is a skill—you get better mainly through practice. Sure, there some few people gifted with the ability to write without much practice, but the odds are that you are not one of them. We have to learn this skill. Even if you have mastered the nuts and bolts of composition—grammar, punctuation, and vocabulary—you still need to think about your use of the language. Learning how to write well takes time and a degree of self-examination. It is mainly to help you in your self-examination that the following guidelines are offered.

Aids to Writing

There are certain things you ought to have on your desk. An absolute minimum is a good dictionary. If you are writing using a computer, have a Web site dictionary running and minimized while you write. You will be surprised how often you use it. A close second is a book on English style; a third, perhaps, is a good thesaurus (there are combination dictionary/thesaurus Web sites). To these you can add the various books related to your classes.

The Dictionary   The best dictionary is one that is up to date and complete enough to include all the nontechnical words you are likely to want to understand, use, or spell. We have already listed a few of the dictionaries that are useful to have (they are often called "desk dictionaries" for good reason).

No matter which one you choose, it will not be of much help unless you get in the habit of using it. Before the days of handheld computer spellers and spell-check programs on computers, students used the dictionary most often to check spelling. You still need a dictionary for that, but a far more important use of the dictionary is as a source of information about the meanings and usage of words. One of the best ways to educate yourself is to become a definition hunter. By looking up words you don't know or words that seem to be used in strange ways, you will greatly increase your ability in the most widely used intellectual commodity of our time, the ability to read and to write.

Style Guides   Besides the dictionary, you probably ought to have a handy reference on grammar, usage, and punctuation. There are many books of this type, but one of the best is Fred Obrecht's *Minimum Essentials of English*. This small manual summarizes the basic rules of usage, grammar and syntax, style, and hints on effective writing. Strunk and White's *Elements of Style* (referred to before) and the *Chicago Manual of Style* are larger and considered the definitive voice on style. If you are concerned about organization in your writing, there is nothing better than Christenson and Christenson's *A New Rhetoric*. Any of these books will answer most of your questions about composition, and they will help you avoid the common mistakes college students make in writing.

The Thesaurus   Peter Mark Roget was a nineteenth-century physician who loved words. He compiled *A Thesaurus of the English Language,* based on a system that he invented for classifying all of human knowledge. Like Webster's *Dictionary,* his work has long been copied by others, sometimes well and sometimes not. But in nearly all thesauruses, the most useful section gives a comprehensive list of synonyms—words with similar meanings—and antonyms—words with opposite meanings. Referring to these lists may help you pick just the right word when that is a critical matter. Many writers swear by it. A similar work built on different principles is *Webster's Dictionary of Synonyms*.

How far you go in developing a personal collection of aids to writing will depend partly on how much money you have to spend and partly on your interests. If you are going to major in a subject in the humanities or in the social sciences where you would be required to write more papers than if you majored in the natural sciences, you will probably want at least some of the basic references we have mentioned. But whatever you acquire, use them.

Basic Aids   If you find reading this book difficult, then you need more help than the above suggestions provide. But more to the point, you probably need personal help. You may have a unique problem with written language that only a one-on-one diagnosis can solve.

Developing Good Writing

The main difference between good writing and bad writing is that good writing says exactly what the author intends. Some writing, of course, has a literary as well as an informative purpose. But for most of us, writing informative prose clearly, accurately, and simply is enough.

Sentences   Good writing consists of clear sentences arranged in paragraphs. With this in mind, look carefully and critically at your first draft. You will have to ask yourself: "Have I said exactly what I want to say? Have I said it in the simplest and most direct way?" Then you will want to examine your draft for faults. Here are some of the most common faults in sentences:

   1. The sentence fragment. "High school and college are very different. First the demands that college makes." The second "sentence" is not a sentence but a fragment. It consists of a subject "the demands" and a subordinate clause "that college makes." There is no verb. We don't know whether the writer intended "Here are the demands that college makes," or "The demands that college makes are greater." Sentence fragments can be used effectively (Mark Twain was a master of them), but you must know what you are doing. Most of the time, for most of us, they are to be avoided.

   2. The run-on sentence. "The party was a roaring success, empty cans and paper plates were scattered everywhere." Here, two complete sentences are incorrectly spliced together by a comma. The easiest correction is to replace the comma with a semicolon. Also there are a number of ways to correct this sentence depending on what the writer meant. "The party was a roaring success, but empty cans and paper plates were scattered everywhere," in which case the separate clauses of a compound sentence are joined by a coordinating conjunction ("but"). Or possibly the writer simply meant to set down two unrelated sentences: "The party was a roaring success. Empty cans and paper plates were scattered everywhere." Or maybe the writer intended one of the clauses to be subordinate: "Because the party was such a roaring success, empty cans and paper plates were scattered everywhere."

3. Lack of agreement between subject and verb. "Each of us plan to go." The simple subject of that sentence, "each," is singular, and so the verb should be in the singular form: "Each of us plans to go." Writers commonly make this error when the subject phrase contains both singular and plural nouns. In that case, you need to find the simple subject (what the sentence is really about) and see whether it is singular or plural. Incidentally, the word "none" as a simple subject generally takes a singular verb.

4. Lack of agreement between pronoun and antecedent. "Each person on the team did their best." The use of "their" to replace the awkward locution "he or she" or "his or her" has become common. You hear it from people who should know better—you even see it in newspapers. It is still an error. It is better to reword the sentence to avoid the lack of agreement: "The team members did their best."

5. Dangling or misplaced modifiers. A typical case of a dangling modifier is one in which the modifier or participle modifies the wrong noun as in "Having finally found our seats, the game had already started." The sentence implies that it was the game that had found the seats. Clearly the author meant something like: "The game had already started when we finally found our seats."

Another error similar in nature is one in which an elliptical construction (one in which an element is implied rather that actually stated in the sentence) results in a dangling modifier. For example: "While still rehearsing, Nancy arrived." The author meant, "While we were still rehearsing, Nancy arrived." Elliptical constructions are useful, but you must be careful to make your meaning clear.

6. Trivial errors. There are many mistakes that are not important in themselves (because they don't distort the meaning), but they identify you as an uneducated person. The confusion between "there," "their," and "they're" is an example. "To," "two," and "too"; "for," "four," and "fore"; "bow" (front of a boat), "bow" (tie), and "bough" (on a tree); "sight," "site," and "cite"; "roll" and "role"; "principle" and "principal"; "affect" and "effect"; "advise" and "advice"; "plain" and "plane" are others. English is full of such things. Most of us know better, but sometimes one of these will slip by. Be sure to read your work carefully, especially since a spell-check program on your computer won't catch these kinds of errors.

While we are on the subject, the words "data" and "phenomena" are both plural nouns. The singular for "data" is "datum" and for "phenomena" is "phenomenon." The data/datum error has been around a long time, and one hears educated people say "this data." People in all walks of life misuse "phenomena," so much so that it is likely to become standard usage as a singular word—but this hasn't happened yet.

Most errors can be detected by paying careful attention to the logic of the sentences you write. But in addition to correcting such errors, you can improve your style by avoiding the passive voice where the active voice will do, by varying the kinds of sentences you write, and by eliminating wordy and awkward constructions.

Paragraphs   A paragraph is a collection of sentences that are related but separate. Every paragraph should have a *topic sentence*. The topic sentence should contain the main idea of the paragraph. Every other sentence in the paragraph should develop, explain, or modify that main idea, or be a transitional sentence to the next paragraph. Most of the time the topic sentence comes first. That makes sense because then the reader knows what the paragraph is about. Sometimes for effect the writer will place the topic sentence at the end of the paragraph. If you do that, make sure that you are in control—your readers may get the wrong idea about what you are trying to say.

Sometimes you will want to pull together everything you have said in a paragraph in a *summary sentence*. You may often use a summary sentence as a transition to the next paragraph. By tying together the beginning and the end of a paragraph and relating it to the next paragraph, you can make your writing clear and easy to follow.

What we have said about paragraphs applies to larger segment of your writing. For example, the first paragraph of a paper can serve as the topic statement of the paper, and the paragraph at the beginning of a section can tell what the section is about.

Two Sample Paragraphs and Their Analyses

(From an essay on Sinclair Lewis)

This mastery of the art of description is evident in *Main Street,* which portrays a small, provincial town in minute detail. Lewis was an acute observer of people and places, with a keen ear for the vernacular of the Middle West. He drew heavily on his own background: Will Kennicott's office in Gopher Prairie was a replica of Dr. E. J. Lewis' office in Sauk Centre, the social work of the Thanatopsis Club—establishing the rest room for farmers' wives, the anti-fly campaign, tree planting—was drawn from the activities of Lewis's stepmother, an active club-woman. The character of Carol and her reaction to Gopher Prairie is in many ways modeled on that of Lewis's first wife, Grace Hegger, and her view of Sauk Centre.

— Transitional sentence
— Topic sentence

Explanation and elaboration

(From an essay on the Missouri Compromise)

If New England opposition to slave representation was the major irritant in the growth of the sectional hostility which broke out in 1819–1821, there were others as well. Over the years there had grown up in the South a distinct anti-Yankee sentiment, in part aggravated by the trading practices of Yankee peddlers in the Southern states. This sentiment was given sharp utterance when the disastrous effects of the Panic of 1819 were felt south of the Potomac. In searching for reasons for their distress, it was easy for Southerners to find in such measures as the Tariff of 1816, internal improvement schemes, and the Second Bank of the United States convenient scapegoats. The exuberant nationalism which had followed the close of the war and had caused the Southerners to support these measures was forgotten, and a sober second thought convinced most of the South that thes North was being favored at its expense.

— Topic sentence

Examples and elaboration

Writing good paragraphs calls for order and logic. That is why outlining is useful. It helps you organize your paper into tight, well-constructed units that carry your readers along smoothly and enable them to grasp your meaning.

If you make writing good paragraphs second nature, then you can concentrate on other aspects of your writing–style and rhetoric. To help you appreciate what well-organized paragraphs are like, we have provided an analysis of two sample paragraphs above.

Grammar and Usage   Good writing is based upon a sense for the grammar of the language, and rules for grammar come from good writing and speaking. Moreover, grammar is appropriate to the occasion. There are different levels of grammatical usage. A sentence such as "It sure ain't a real friendly dog" is clear and easy to understand. It would not, however, be appropriate in formal standard English. Most educated people can use their language at different levels. They can speak colloquially when the occasion demands it, and they can speak formally as well. They can vary their writing also, but probably not as easily. This ability to move back and forth appropriately among the various levels of colloquial and formal English is one of the marks of an educated person.

Standard English varies in level. *Informal English* is more often used in speaking than in writing. It is the way educated people talk in informal situations where slang, local idioms, and well-controlled deviations from Standard English are appropriate. *General English* is the kind of language educated people use in more formal conversations, in business letters, and in talks or in articles for general audiences. *Formal English* is more often written than spoken, and it is what you will find in technical writing and academic books.

Most of your writing should be in general Standard English. Avoid a formal style for most of your writing. It sounds stilted, and, unless you are an unusually good writer, it is hard to write it clearly and accurately. Be sure you know the main rules of standard grammar of English and how to use them in a sensible way. If you ignore the basic rules of English, you make your writing illogical and hard to read. What is more, you appear to be ignorant.

What are these basic rules? We can't take the space here to go over them, but we have some questions to test your grasp of grammar. If you have a hard time answering them, you owe yourself a review of the fundamentals.

Can you identify the subject of a sentence? Do you know the difference between the phrase containing the subject and the simple subject? Do you know what a direct object is? A prepositional phrase? Can you identify the nominative, objective, and possessive cases of pronouns? Do you know what the "principle parts of a verb" means, and can you identify them for regular and irregular verbs?

Do you fall into some of the common traps awaiting you in the language? One of these is the use of the irregular verbs "lay" and "lie." If you wrote, "He laid there for some time" you would be showing confusion. "Laid" is the past tense of "to lay" and not the past tense of "to lie." (If you don't know the difference between these two verbs, look them up in a dictionary or handbook.)

The past tense of the verb "lie" is "lay," so the sentence should read, "He lay there for some time."

Mistakes such as this one are not terribly important by themselves; they seldom interfere with your ability to say what you mean. Nevertheless, they show that you do not understand the English language as well as an educated person should. The real purpose in studying grammar is not to avoid trivial mistakes but to help you write good Standard English. Trivial errors are symptomatic of your level of ability in using the language. If you make too many such errors, the chances are that you can't identify such important parts of a sentence such as the subject, the direct object, the object of a preposition, the indirect object, and auxiliary verbs. Even more important, the chances are that you will not be able to correct an error once you have made one.

Get in the habit of carefully reading what you write so that you can correct your own mistakes. When your instructor corrects something on your paper, make sure you know what the correct form is and why you made the error. If you don't know why you made a mistake or why you were corrected, find out. Obrecht's *Minimum Essentials of English* will help you do this.

Punctuation   Good punctuation is essential to clear writing. You can punctuate properly just by knowing a few rules and applying common sense.

Periods

The period is the basic punctuation mark. You use it to show that an idea together with its modifiers is complete. How do you know when you have written a complete idea? Think about how you talk. Your intonation changes, and very likely you will pause at the end of an idea. This is where you would normally put a period.

Commas

The use of commas is more difficult than the use of periods because there are many more uses for them. Following are the most common uses for commas:

1. An idea that depends on another. "If it rains, the picnic will be postponed." The first idea, the subordinate clause, is separated from the second idea, the main clause by a comma.

2. Two main ideas connected by a coordinating conjunction. The comma goes before the conjunction as in: "Jerry got a new stereo, but he left it at home."

3. Items listed in a series. "I'm taking economics, psychology, French, and physics."

4. A main clause and a parenthetical expression. "No one, you will be happy to know, flunked the exam."

5. Noun phrases and their nonrestrictive appositives. "Bill, my oldest brother, is getting married in the fall."

6. The parts of dates. For example, "December 25, 2002," or "Monday, June 24, 2003."

7. Titles or names in direct address. "I'm calling, Sue, to invite you to my birthday party." "Excuse me, professor, but I think you are wrong."

8. Nonrestrictive relative clauses. "John, who was the last to leave, got stuck with the bill." Restrictive clauses are not set off by commas: "The person who was the last to leave got stuck with the bill." Notice that in the latter case, the relative clause identifies the person—it is essential to the meaning of the sentence—while in the former case, the relative just tells you something incidental about John—that he was the last to leave.

This list does not exhaust the uses of commas, but it does give you some of the more important and common ones. Furthermore, there are some minor differences among style manuals concerning comma usage.

Finally we have said nothing about parentheses, quotation marks (either single or double), colons, semicolons, question marks, and exclamation points. If you think that you need some help with any of these, consult one of the manuals mentioned earlier. Also many dictionaries have a section on current usage.

Spelling   As a college student, you are expected to spell correctly *all* the words you use. Here are some ways to ensure that you do:

1. Be careful. Many misspellings are the result of haste and carelessness. Proofread. Do everything you can to make sure that mistakes in spelling are not just the result of misplaced fingers on the keyboard.

2. Pay attention to the spelling of new words and names. If you are not the kind of person who can look at a new word and be able to spell it immediately, practice writing or imagining how you would write new words.

3. Use the dictionary.

4. Use your spell-check program.

5. Get to know a few simple rules (*i* before *e* except after *c* when the sound is eee). Look for special endings. Find rules for spelling in grammar books and dictionaries.

Most instructors resent poor spelling. It makes them think that either you are illiterate or you don't care enough to put the effort into spelling. If you know you are weak in spelling, invest in something that will enable you to spell properly. The best advice is to be alert to your language. In English you can't always depend on the sounds of the words: Know that if I *choose* my team carefully, I may *lose* the game anyway. Above all, keep a good dictionary handy.

Vocabulary   A typical college student "knows" about 160,000 words. That means the student can understand in context that many words although he or she may not be able to give a precise definition. Of course, the typical student actually uses fewer words. If your vocabulary is too small to express your ideas, you need to improve your vocabulary.

Being in the habit of using a dictionary is the biggest aid in building your vocabulary. But learning the dictionary definitions, or *denotations,* of words will not necessarily help you understand their *connotations.* The connotation of a word is the meaning it suggests in addition to its literal meaning. For example, using the word "slender" to describe someone connotes approval; whereas "skinny" connotes disapproval, and "scrawny" has an even more negative connotation. "Assertive" is usually a neutral word (or slightly positive), but "pushy" is always negative. The more aware you are of words' connotations, the more precisely you will be able to convey your attitudes through your writing. The best way to learn the connotations of words is to read, read, read. Read everything. Read always.

One of the most common faults in students' writing is the use of big words when simple words would do better. Why say, "The methodology employed in this investigation is factor analysis," when you could say, "We used factor analysis in this investigation."

Avoid jargon words such as "finalize;" use "complete" instead. The word "parameters" is often misused (most often to mean limits). Avoid it unless you mean it in its precise mathematical sense. Avoid euphemisms such as "passed away" for "died" and "intoxicated" for "drunk." Above all, be careful about the use of such all-purpose verbs such as "involve."

Another fault is wordiness—using several words where one or two would do. Instead of saying, "In spite of the fact that it snowed, we went ahead with the party anyway," say, "We went ahead with the party despite the snow." Instead of, "He did his work in a careless manner," say, "He worked carelessly." Instead of, "She is a person who likes everyone," say, "She likes everyone." When you revise your compositions, simplify wordy constructions when you see them.

Reading a lot is a good way to improve your vocabulary. Make an effort to read things that are well written. Ask yourself as you read why the writing is good or why it is bad. Try your hand at editing someone else's writing. Many of the things you read could be better written. Everyone knows how badly written government documents can be. See if you can improve what you find in one of them. You may never be one of the great stylists of all time, but if you can write a technical report, a stockholder's statement, or a new government regulation so that it can easily be understood by literate people, you will have achieved one of the main purposes of your education.

Studying a Foreign Language

C H A P T E R

8

Two subjects seem to divide students into two groups: those who can and those who can't. These subjects are foreign languages and mathematics. You have to approach studying these subjects differently from the way you do other subjects because they require a lot of concentrated effort to master. They are, however, very different in their demands, and so we have separate chapters for each of them. Learning a foreign language takes practice and, for most people, a fair amount of rote memorization.

There are a few people who have no trouble learning foreign languages. There are famous scholars who have *taught themselves* 20 or 30 different languages. But nearly all the rest of us have some trouble learning a foreign language because the task requires so many different skills. If you find reading a new language easy, you may have difficulty understanding the spoken language. Many people who can read and write other languages easily have a tin ear and just can't hear—much less speak—the unfamiliar vowel sounds of German, French, or Swedish. Even if you get through the hurdles of grammar and drill, you may find that you just can't think in Italian. Or you may be able to understand sentences in Russian but just can't find the way to put them in English. Find out for yourself those things you can do well and those that give you trouble. If you identify those things you do well, you can use them to help you over the troublesome parts. If you can't seem to get a hold anywhere in a foreign language, you will have to work extra hard. The purpose of this chapter is to give you some ideas for making your study of languages as efficient and pleasant as possible.

BASIC RULES FOR LEARNING A LANGUAGE

Keep Up with the Work

Steve runs on the varsity cross-country team. Every day, rain or shine, hot or cold, he runs at least 7 miles. He wouldn't think of missing a day's practice. Even a bad cold can't keep him off the course, and he once ran 10 miles with an infected splinter in his foot.

Steve also takes French I. He approaches French with a little less dedication. Twice he overslept and missed class. Once he had to miss class to go on a cross-country meet at another school. The week he had a cold, he felt too rotten to go to class. French is his least favorite subject, so he puts off studying it until the last possible minute. The result is that he squeaks by with a marginal D. Even if he passes, the chances are that he will have to repeat it before he is ready to go on to the next level.

It has never occurred to Steve that the attitudes and habits that make him a good long-distance runner would also make him a good French student if he gave the language half a chance. If he went after French the way he goes after running, he could be an A student.

You may fall behind in economics, history, literature, or even chemistry and catch up—though we don't recommend it. If you fall behind in a foreign language, however, you've had it. Regular attendance and regular daily preparations are not just desirable; they are absolutely necessary in learning a foreign language.

Learning a language is cumulative. Everything you learn later depends upon what you have already learned. You have to know the meanings of words before you can put them together in phrases and sentences. You have to know how to pronounce the sounds and hear them accurately before you can talk to and understand a native speaker. You have to know about word order in the new language before you can understand anything but the simplest of sentences. You have to know how verbs are conjugated and how nouns and adjectives are declined before you can make sense out of the simplest of stories.

It takes dedicated practice. You know that if you work out at tennis one day a week, you will never make the tennis team. With a foreign language you must practice regularly to be even moderately successful at learning that language. You must learn the simple things well enough so that you can use them in understanding the complicated things.

Spend Lots of Time in Recitation

Recitation both in class and in study is basic to learning a new language. The easiest way to fail a foreign language course is never to recite. At least 80 percent of your study time, particularly in the early stages of language learning, should be spent in recitation. What is more, you need to recite on a daily basis—every single day, not just 3 days a week right before class.

There are three skills you learn in acquiring a new language. First, you must learn to read it. Second, you should learn to understand it when you hear it. Third, you should learn to speak it. Americans are notoriously behind many other countries in learning other languages. Most Europeans, for example, speak two languages at least; whereas we Americans generally are not too good at the one language we speak—our native language. If you are thinking about running for Congress in the Southwest, you had better speak Spanish, or you are lost before you start. If the only language you know is English, you are the poorer for it, and learning a foreign language is worth at least as much effort as you put into your tennis or golf game or into being a passable pianist. Like these things, learning a new language is a *skill*. Even if you only want to learn to read, you have to practice. And practice means recitation and translation as the most important step. But in order to recite and translate, you need to master the grammar and acquire a vocabulary in your new language.

Master the Grammar

Most American college courses in a foreign language at the beginner's level stress grammar. Language teachers want you to know the structure of the language you are studying. If you know the rules of grammar in a language, you can construct sentences of your own in that language, and you can understand what people say to you.

One problem with teaching grammar in a foreign language is that many students have either forgotten or never learned the rudiments of English grammar. When they hear about tense, mood, gerunds, participles, and cases in Spanish, French, or Russian, they have no idea what the teacher is talking about. If you find yourself in this spot, try to make up your deficiencies as you go along. You can do this with a handbook of English grammar. (A couple of which are mentioned earlier.) Another way is to "translate back" into English. Find out what the equivalent of the Russian or Spanish nominative is in English. In fact, many people find that learning a foreign language this way—mastering the grammar of the language—is a good way to come to a deep understanding of English grammar.

Few students of English grammar will have encountered expressions such as "a noun in the dative case" or "an accusative pronoun." The reason is that among European languages, English is unusual. It depends much more upon word order to express grammatical meaning than upon other things such as word endings. In most other European languages the endings do what word order does in English. In Latin, for example, the word for girl is "*puella*." Thus you would say, "*Puella puerum amat*" (The girl loves the boy). But if you wanted to say, "The boy loves the girl," you would change the "*-a*" ending in "*puella*" to "*-am*." You would most likely say, "*Puer puellam amat*." You would change the ending because "girl" is now in the accusative case rather than in the nominative. Because of the dependence upon word endings, most Latin sentences can be written in different word orders (though typically in simple sentences the verb is last). In English, the order is all-important. (Think about "The boy loves the girl" and "The girl loves the boy.")

Whenever you run across an unfamiliar grammatical term while studying a foreign language, make sure you understand it. If it has an equivalent in English or a near equivalent, make sure you know what the comparable English construction would be. Some grammatical terms, such as "aspect," are rarely used in English (though it does exist in English), but don't just throw up your hands when you hear about aspect in Russian. Find out what it means.

When you become skilled in the language, you will realize that the grammatical categories have a meaning all their own, and you won't need English as a crutch. If you are studying German, you should be able to rattle off the declensions of German nouns—nominative, "*das Haus;*" accusative, "*das Haus;*" genitive, "*das Hauses;*" dative, "*dem Hause*." And you should understand how they are used in German sentences.

All languages are full of irregularities—exceptions to general rules and bafflingly contrary rules covering only a few words. These have to be learned by brute force—just memorize them. Although grammarians try to discover rules that will apply as widely as possible, there are always exceptions. If you think that French, German, or Russian are maddeningly irregular, you should count your blessings that you are not learning English as a second language. It is far and away the most irregular of all of the European languages.

In all languages the words that are most frequently used tend to be irregular or retain ancient forms. Consider conjugating the verb "to be." The simple present and past tenses of this verb are: I am, you are, he/she/it is; we are, you are, they are; I was, you were, he/she/it was; we were, you were, they were. Contrast that with: I walk, you walk, he/she/it walks; we walk, you walk, they walk; I walked, you walked, they walked. There are only two rules for "walk": add "-s" to form the third person singular (she walks) and add "-ed" to form the past tense. The only thing you can do with irregular verbs is to memorize them, recite them, and use them in the context of simple sentences. They have to become as second nature to you as putting one foot in front of the other in walking.

Language teachers stress grammar because it is the main tool we have for mastering a language when we have a lot of other things to do. You didn't learn to speak English (or whatever your native language is) by learning the rules of grammar. Most people learn the basics of their native tongue between ages 1 to 5. They didn't learn it by going to class 3 or 4 hours per week and practicing it for another 8 to 10 hours; they learned it by being immersed in it all their waking hours. And even then, a 5-year-old still has a long way to go to be able to speak the language like an adult. If you are a college freshman, it took you about 18 years to achieve the mastery of English you have today. Since you don't have 18 years to learn the new language, the best thing to do is to learn the grammatical rules and *practice* reading, listening, and speaking.

Learning Unusual Languages

The world is expanding, and, while most of you will choose a familiar European language as a second language to learn, some of you will tackle Thai, Arabic, Classical Greek, or Chinese. Most of these languages will not use the alphabet that is familiar to you–the Roman alphabet. Greek, Russian, Arabic, Thai, and Amharic all use different alphabets. Some languages such as Japanese and Chinese do not use an alphabet at all. If you are studying one of these languages, the most important step is to learn the code–the notation. If you can't decode the printed symbols, you will be lost even if you have a good ear for the sounds of the language.

Many of these languages have an exotic grammar. English is exotic, but it is at least close enough to the more familiar European languages for us to latch onto grammatical landmarks in learning the new language. But Chinese and Japanese are so different grammatically that most of the familiar landmarks are gone. In learning Chinese, for example, you will have to work harder than your classmates who are studying French or German in order to master the equivalent level. Get used to the idea that you are going to be much more on your own.

Learn to Think in the Language

You know that you have really mastered another language when you can think in that language. To think in a language means not only that you are fluent in it, but also that you don't have to translate. You don't read English by translating; that is, you don't turn words into other words in order to understand. You know directly what each word means. You don't have to think about it. That's the goal you need to work toward in studying another language. Right from the beginning, you should try to associate foreign words not with their English equivalents but directly with the objects, events, and qualities they name. As you become more skillful in your new language, you will find that you think in it without having to refer to the English equivalents.

LEARNING TO READ THE LANGUAGE

At first you will be tempted to translate, but you should resist that temptation. Learning to think in a new language is a gradual process, but you won't give it a chance if you don't try to think in the new language from the outset. As you go from one level to the next, you may find some of the following hints helpful.

Studying by Phrases and Sentences

Whatever you do, don't try word-for-word translation. That will get you in trouble right from the start, and, as the material gets more complicated, it becomes a hopeless task. This is especially true with languages such as Latin and German in which the word order is different from that in English. Second-year students in German will easily get lost if they try to find their way through a sentence word by word. One of the problems is that German has separable verbs, and they really provide traps for word-by-word translation. In separable verbs, the prefix may be detached from the verb and moved to the end of the sentence. If you try to translate the stem of the verb without its prefix, you will be translating the wrong word. But even in languages such as French, in which the word order is very much like that in English, you will find it much better to try to grasp the meaning of the whole phrase or the whole sentence. It will seem strange and unnatural at first, but once you get used to it, it will become the only way you will attack new sentences in a foreign language.

If, after a semester or two of a new language, you are still translating word by word, you need help. You might discuss the problem with your instructor. It may be that you haven't memorized the basic elements of the vocabulary such as relative pronouns or irregular verbs. These together with auxiliary verbs and prepositions have to be second nature to you. You have to recognize them instantly when you see them in a sentence, and you have to know what they mean immediately.

Perhaps you don't know the syntax or word order well enough to be able to tell where you are in a sentence. For example, take the German sentence, "*Haben sie den Bauer gesehen, der auf dem Wagen sass?*" ("Have you seen the farmer who was sitting on the wagon?") A badly confused student may try to translate "*der*" as a definite article ("the") rather than as a relative pronoun ("who"). This mistake would result from translating the sentence word by word rather than trying to see the syntax pattern. A parallel problem in French is illustrated by the sentence "*Elle a reçu les fleurs que lui ont envoyées des amies*" ("She received the flowers that friends sent her"), where the unobservant student may read the objective pronoun "*que*" ("that") as the nominative pronoun "*qui*" ("who"), which makes no sense. If you look over the whole sentence and relate the words one to another, you will not make mistakes such as these.

Looking Up Words: Some Dos and Don'ts

A common mistake students make when trying to translate is to look up too many words. There are two things wrong with this.

First, you may not have to look up the word if you read on and get the context in which the word is used. This is what we do when we read something unfamiliar in English. Consulting a dictionary is only one way of learning the meaning of a word, and it is time-consuming and sometimes ineffective because it isolates the meaning from the context in which the word is used. Most of the words we know in English we learned from their context. Context always limits the kinds of words that can appear in particular places in sentences. Because of this limitation, you can often guess the meaning of a word.

Second, you often find more than one meaning for a word in a dictionary. You will only know which meaning is correct by the context in which the word appears.

Thus, try to guess the meaning from the context. If you are puzzled, consult a dictionary. Don't just stop when you get to a word you don't know; read the whole sentence and try to figure it out. Keep the number of words that you look up to a minimum. Even if you make the wrong guess, something in the succeeding sentences will more than likely tell you that you have made a mistake.

If you have to look up a word, mark it in some way so that you will know that it is a word that was unfamiliar to you. Then make sure that you can place the word in the context of the sentence correctly.

Another thing: Always reread a passage soon after you have translated it for the first time. This way you can spot trouble and you become more familiar with the words that baffled you in the first place.

Dissecting Words

The time and place for paying attention to individual words is (1) when you have to read a sentence and can't get its meaning because you're not sure about one or more words in it, and (2) when you want to build your vocabulary.

While learning a language, you are continuously adding to your store of usable words. You will save yourself a lot of work if you learn how to break down words into their elements. We comment on this in the section on building your English vocabulary, but this advice is perhaps even more significant in the study of another language.

Languages are put together in different ways, but most of them are like English in that they have root words or stems to which prefixes and suffixes may be attached. If you learn the general meaning of the prefixes and suffixes (collectively known as affixes), you can often figure out a word you have never seen before just by dissecting it. In English, you know that the prefix "pre-" means before. Whenever you see "pre-" at the beginning of a word, you can tell that the word pertains to something going on before, as in premeditation, prelude, or premonition. It's much the same way in other languages, and even though there may seem to be a lot of affixes because of all the combinations they can produce, there are usually relatively few of them to be learned.

Some languages, such as German, have many compound words. These are words in which the elements are not necessarily affixes and root but may be two or more whole words glued together. Thus, the German word "*Durchgangsgerechtigkeit*" means "right-of-way" or "thoroughfare," and it is compounded out of several separate words and affixes. If you study advanced German, you will have to learn how to dissect words because many of the words you run across will not be in the dictionary. The person who wrote them simply made them up by compounding existing words.

Using Cognates

Many words in other European languages resemble words in English with the same or similar meanings. That is because English has roots in both Germanic and Romance languages. Moreover, English words were either directly borrowed from Latin or Greek or were coined by using Latin or Greek roots: For example, coaxial, fission, and interstellar are from Latin; economics, drama, biology, and cyclotron are from Greek. Some English words have even been borrowed from Hindi, Russian, and Yiddish.

Although words that are imported from another language may have been altered somewhat in the process, there is often a perceptible relation between the original and the imported word. If you learn to recognize such similar words, called "cognates," you will find translation to be much easier. To get an idea of what we mean, try the exercise we have provided on pages 156–158. (You don't have to know the languages other than English to do the exercise—in fact it is better if you don't.) You will find that you can guess the meanings of many words in other languages you have not studied.

You must be careful, however. Cognates can lead you astray in some cases. Sometimes strange things happen in the process of a word moving from one language to another. "*Le crayon*" does not mean crayon in French; it means pencil. The English word "black" is historically related to the French word "*blanc*," which means white! Even when the meanings of cognate words are similar (as in "*crayon*" and "crayon"), there may be fine shades of difference between them that you can't easily detect. It is a good rule, therefore, to look up such words and check their meaning. But do this only after you have attempted a guess based on their similarity to English. Identifying cognates helps make the study process an active one.

Using Cards

Studying a language takes a lot of memorizing. A good technique for making memorizing easier is to write the foreign word on one side of a card and its translation on the other side. In fact you may buy cards like this, but it is far better if you prepare your own (active participation again). You can test yourself by running thorough the foreign words while making translations of them. Whenever you're stumped or you're not sure, you can flip over the card to get the correct answer.

Use of Cognates

Here are two translations of an earlier edition of *How to Study,* one in French and one in Spanish. Even if you don't know French or Spanish, read through them and underline any word that resembles a word in English. Most of these words will be cognates; that is to say, they will be related to and will mean the same or similar things as English words. A few will be what the French call "false friends." These are words that resemble English words but mean different things. We have provided a list of words that resemble one another in English and French and in English and Spanish, together with the correct English translations. Check the words you underlined against the list, and be sure to note the correct translations. This exercise will show you how helpful hunting for similar words can be in understanding some of the familiar European languages.

The French translation, *Comment Étudier,* was adapted from the English by André Roy and published in 1968 by McGraw-Hill Éditeurs, Montreal, Canada. The Spanish translation, *Como Estudiar,* was published in 1967 by Editorial Magisterio Español, S.A., Madrid, Spain.

Usage de fiches de vocabulaire

La technique qui suit s'est révélée efficace pour l'acquisition du vocabulaire. Lorsque vous rencontrez un mot moins familier, inscrivez-le au recto d'une fiche avec sa signification au verso; revisez ces fiches chaque jour, pointez-les chaque foi que vous vous souvenez du sens du mot et inscrivez un zéro chaque fois que vous devez regarder au verso pour vous rafraîchir la mémoire. Quand vous aurez pointé la fiche cinq fois sans aucun zéro, vous pourrez considérer que vous connaissez ce mot et vous jetterez la carte, évitant ainsi d'en accumuler un trop grand nombre. (page 74)

French Word	Similar English Word	English Translation
usage	usage	use
technique	technique	technique
suit	suit	follows
révélée	reveal	revealed, shown
efficace	efficacious	efficacious
pour	pour	for
acquisition	acquisition	acquisition
vocabulaire	vocabulary	vocabulary
rencontrez	encounter	meet with
familier	familiar	familiar
inscrivez	inscribe	inscribe, set down
signification	significance	significance

Use of Cognates (*Continued*)

French Word	Similar English Word	English Translation
revisez	revise	revise
pointez	point	mark, check
souvenez	souvenir	remember, recall
sens	sense	meaning
zéro	zero	zero
regarder	regard	look at
refraîcher	refresh	refresh
mémoire	memory	memory
considérer	consider	consider
jetterez	jettison	throw away
carte	card	card
accumuler	accumulate	accumulate
grand	grand	large
nombre	number	number

Uso de las fichas

Como ya hemos indicado, en el estudio de los idiomas hay que ejercitar mucho la memoria, y los estudiantes han probado un gran número de técnicas para hacerlo más fácil y eficaz. Una técnica muy empleada es escribir una palabra extranjera en la cara de una ficha y su traducción en la otra cara. (Desde luego, puedes comprar tales fichas ya impresas.) Puedes autoexaminarte mirando las palabras extranjeras y viendo las que sabes traducir. Cuando llegues a una cuyo significado no recuerdes, no tienes más que dar la vuelta a la ficha. Esta puede ser una práctica eficaz si se usa juiciosamente. (page 163)

Spanish Word	Similar English Word	English Translation
uso	use	use
indicado	indicate	appropriate, advisable
en	in	at, in, into, by, on
estudio	studio, study	study
idiomas	idioms	language, idiom
mucho	much	much, a lot of
memoria	memory	memory
estudiantes	students	students
probado	prove	test, try, prove

Use of Cognates (*Continued*)

Spanish Word	Similar English Word	English Translation
un	one	one, a
gran	grand	big, large, great
numéro	numeral	number
técnicas	technical	technique
empleada	employ	employ, use
escribir	inscribe	write
extranjera	extraneous	foreign
traducción	translation	translation
otra	other	other, another
comprar	compare	buy, purchase
tales	tales	such, such a
impresos	impress	printed
autoexaminarte	self-examination	self-examine
traducir	traduce	translate
significado	significant	meaning
no	no	not, no
eficaz	efficacy	efficacious, efficient
juiciosamente	judicious	judiciously
práctica	practice	method, skill

Making up your own cards will help you with spelling foreign words as well as providing you with recitation. Keep your working stack of cards small. Make sure you have mastered your initial set before you add new cards. When you are absolutely sure of a word, remove it from the working stack.

When you begin to translate more difficult passages, it's a good idea to make a card for every word you have to look up. Go over these at set intervals, perhaps once a day. Each time you remember what the word means, put a check mark on the card, and each time you don't, put a zero. When you have five check marks on a card without a zero, remove the card from the stack.

Another way of using cards is to write down whole phrases, not just single words. These help you to think in larger units and to use words in their proper context. Then too, many phrases are idiomatic and cannot be translated literally on a word-for-word basis. The familiar French phrase "*Comment allez-vous?*" literally means, "How do you go?" but the correct translation is "How are you?"

Many students write the English equivalent of foreign words in the margins or between the lines of passages they are translating. This is not as good as using cards. It sounds easier, but it has two disadvantages. First, it leaves the translation in full view and makes it almost impossible for you to recite without prompting. Second, focusing your attention on the translation keeps you thinking in English rather than in the new language. Since you eventually want to know the meanings of words without connecting them to English, the less you rely on English, the better.

Using Ponies and Trots

If you are in an advanced language class in which you are reading whole books or lengthy excerpts, you may be tempted to buy English translations known as "ponies" or "trots." Some ponies supply English translations between the lines of foreign print. Avoid these at all costs. Aside from distracting you, they keep you from figuring out the meanings of the words, and they distort the foreign syntax. They deprive you of the ability to recite. Sometimes the translations are poor, so you may actually be misled. All in all, they are a real handicap in learning a new language.

In trots, the foreign text is on one page, and the English equivalent is on the opposite page. This arrangement is useful if you want to read a book in a language you have never mastered. However it is a bad idea to use a trot as a study aid. It will slow down and inhibit the learning process. In short, while there are times when it is profitable to read an English translation of something you are going to translate, most of the time it is not.

LEARNING TO SPEAK A FOREIGN LANGUAGE

Much of what we say about learning to read a new language also applies to learning to speak one. In the early stages of learning, the two go hand in hand. Speaking the language helps you learn to read it. If you wish to gain fluency as rapidly as possible, however, you will need to make use of some special techniques.

Total Immersion

You learned to speak English by hearing it spoken and by speaking it yourself. You learned by copying others, inventing on your own, and being corrected, being aware that you weren't saying things quite the same way other people were saying them. By the time you were ready to go to school and long before you could read or write, you had a better mastery of English than a person could acquire by studying it in college for a couple of years. All this happened without your knowing anything about grammar, reading, and writing.

Children are immersed in a world of language. That is how they learn it. Several of the crash programs for teaching people to comprehend and speak a new language in a short time—the Berlitz method, for example—make use of total immersion. However, total immersion is seldom possible for most college students. But even if you can't be part of a total immersion program, you can practice the new language in a variety of situations and use it to think with as much as you can. Seek out native speakers of the language you are studying and get them to talk to you in their native tongue. Read foreign newspapers and magazines. Check out foreign videotapes (with subtitles) and listen to them.

In larger universities there are generally houses or dining rooms devoted to a particular language. If you are studying French, for example, get in the habit of having lunch at the French House.

Imitating

To make a language habitual, you must practice it regularly. One important tool of practice is imitation. This is where language laboratories are important. Almost every institution, however small, maintains language laboratories equipped with listening devices, recording devices, and tapes in at least the common European languages. You will probably be required to log in a certain number of hours in such a lab. If so, exceed the number of required hours. Listening to tapes of native speakers, recording your own speech, and correcting your errors all help you master the spoken language. You learn the rhythm of native speech, and you can experiment with making unfamiliar vowel sounds.

Memorizing

There is no way around it; you have to memorize when you are learning a foreign language as an adult. Imitating itself results in a kind of memorization, but in addition to trying to duplicate what you hear, you must concentrate on remembering words and phrases. Rehearsing over and over again seems to be about the best way to do it. The object is to make certain things so habitual that you don't need to think about them. Then you can concentrate on what you want to say and on new combinations of words.

Studying Out Loud

Language labs are generally designed so that you can speak in response to what you hear. In cubicles that are more or less sound insulated, you can respond to what the instructor says or what you hear on your tapes without embarrassment. But even when you are not in the language lab, read aloud as much as possible. As long as you read silently, you learn the language only visually. To be sure, reading aloud slows you down, but reading assignments, except in advanced classes, are generally short in language departments, so the lost time is worth the effort.

Spacing Studying Time Effectively

In learning something that requires repetitive practice—as learning a foreign language does—spacing the practice is essential for efficient learning. Don't make your study periods too long or too short. Divide an assignment into two parts and master each part separately. Then allow time for rereading and review. Provide for short rest periods. A half-hour is plenty of time if you are reciting out loud. If you break 2 hours of foreign language study into 4 half-hour periods separated by rest or by studying other subjects, you will learn more than if you studied for 2 hours uninterrupted.

IN GENERAL

Some courses emphasize reading the language; others, speaking it. Some stress grammar, while others don't. Some require a very precise understanding of words, while others allow rather free translations and may even encourage it. More commonly in the past (when graduate schools required two foreign languages), larger colleges offered special courses in scientific French and German so that students in the sciences could learn to read the technical literature in those languages. Today, you are more likely to find such courses in Russian or Chinese. Whatever the emphasis of the course you are taking, your instructor will stress those techniques that are most suitable for the particular purpose of that course.

Many schools encourage students of foreign languages to study abroad. If you have the chance to spend a summer, a semester, or even a whole year studying in another country, do so. There is no better way to become familiar with the way other people live and think than to live among them for a while.

We have had little to say about the special problems of learning languages that do not use the Roman alphabet–languages such as Greek, Arabic, and Hebrew–because, relatively speaking, few students take such languages. But the number is increasing, particularly for Japanese, Chinese, Russian, and Hebrew. If you have a talent for learning languages, treat yourself to some courses in one of these languages. Learning one of these languages, the organization of which is generally very different from English, can be one of the most valuable experiences of your college years.

Finally, we need to say an additional word about those people who have real difficulties with foreign languages. While there are differences in aptitudes for learning languages, most people who have trouble learning a language encounter problems either because they do not study enough or because they study in the wrong way. Nowhere, except perhaps in studying mathematics, are good work habits more important than in learning foreign languages. If you do have little aptitude for learning languages, you need to allow more time for studying than most students. But remember, as Mark Twain remarked, even French *babies* learn to speak French.

Computers, Mathematics, and Science

9

$\mathbf{M}$any people have difficulty with various subjects in their academic career, but there are three subjects that frequently generate real phobias. Students will often say that they don't write well or that economics is a bore, but if you mention algebra or trigonometry, they will turn ashen, start to sweat, and complain that they can't do mathematics. They have been putting it off for as long as they can, and now it is time—they must take a course in order to graduate. Or they have to take statistics for their major and realize that they need algebra first, and they just can't do that. Computers are a close second to mathematics in the fear department. Although most students are able to turn on a computer and play games or write using a word processing program, they know that to study computers requires logic and some mathematics background, and they just can't do that. Many students actively search their college catalog looking for the easiest science course that will allow them to graduate; "Rocks for Jocks" is a popular one. Most science courses use mathematics to some extent, some more than others, and students just can't do that.

Do you notice the theme among the three subjects that generate phobias? It's mathematics. If you have made a career of avoiding computer classes, science, and mathematics, you have a lot of company. But even if you belong to this big club, it is one you shouldn't be in. Math phobia is one of the worst handicaps you can have in today's world. Not only do physics, engineering, chemistry, biology, and related fields require mathematics and the tools of scientific thinking, but social sciences such as economics, psychology, and sociology as well as such practical fields such as accounting and business administration use them. Statistics, finite mathematics, linear algebra, and computer programming are all used in modern business management. Even if you are aiming for a major in physical education, literature, art, music, or drama, you can't claim to be an educated person if you are nearly illiterate in mathematics, as some students are. The sooner you face up to your deficiencies in mathematics and science, the better off you will be.

Many third graders know how to use computers. The level of skill you acquire for using computers depends what you use them for, but some basic skill is absolutely required. There are courses now that are conducted entirely on a computer, including the examinations. And now some colleges routinely supply a computer and associated software for every student enrolled. We think that to use the modern computer efficiently, you should know how to touch-type. Using your computers for homework, term papers, and course projects is essential.

If you think you can get by without understanding basic mathematics, consider the case of Anne. She graduated with a strong record and a major in English from one of the country's most prestigious colleges. All through her academic career she concentrated on avoiding courses in mathematics and science. She barely got through ninth-grade algebra and quit doing any mathematics at all just as soon as she could. In college, she fulfilled her science requirement by taking the Rocks for Jocks course that required almost no scientific reasoning and no mathematics whatsoever. Two years after graduating from college, as the result of some job experience and other things, she decided that she wanted to do graduate work in psychology. She discovered that while some quite good graduate schools would be willing to take her without an undergraduate major in psychology, not one of them would let her get by without having studied statistics. She had no recourse but to go back and be tutored in the elementary mathematics she had worked so hard to avoid. There is a postscript to this story: She eventually did so well in advanced statistics that she was asked, during her last year in graduate school, to be a teaching assistant in the computer-based statistics course in the institution's graduate school of business. The moral of this story is that although many people avoid mathematics and the sciences, it is not because they are incapable of doing well; they have just developed a phobia. With proper motivation and good instruction, most people can overcome their fears and remove the roadblocks to successful careers in fields that otherwise would be denied to them. There is no time like the present to begin to correct your mistakes.

COMPUTERS

If, by some miracle, you managed to avoid having to operate a computer in high school, you need to correct this deficiency immediately. Learning to operate a computer, like learning to drive a car, seems more difficult than it really is. (Yes, there are some people who have a phobia about learning to drive a car—the late H. L. Hencken tried, ran into a lamppost, and gave up.)

A computer keyboard is modeled after a typewriter keyboard, but it is much more versatile. Used together with the computer mouse, you can perform editing functions that are impossible with just a typewriter. You can move entire blocks of text around, check spelling and grammar, enter new programs, and save data by various means. There are several additional keys on a computer keyboard called "function keys," each one of which has multiple uses when used by itself or in conjunction with either the "shift," "control," or "alt" keys. And, of course, the most important and useful key on the keyboard is the "backspace" key.

Kinds of Computers

There are two common types of computers in use today, the PC (personal computer), or IBM clones, and the Apples. Which one you get is a personal decision because they both perform pretty much the same functions, although you will find that people get rabid in defending their choice. At your college you may find that the campus is set up to accommodate one type or the other. You should determine whether or not this is true at your college. Most schools have rooms of computers that are linked to the college's "mainframe" (the big computer located in the computer center). They will be loaded with all kinds of programs that you could conceivably want to use. These rooms will also be equipped with state-of-the-art laser printers. In many schools, these rooms are open around the clock, and because they are less likely to be used at, say, two in the morning, many students plan to do their homework or draft a term paper in the middle of the night.

By means of a modem, computers can be hooked up for a fee to either a phone line or a fiber optic cable to be connected to the World Wide Web

(WWW) and the Internet. If you have such a connection, you can do a lot of research right on your computer. Beware. The Internet can be a terrific time waster. It's fun to surf the Internet, and people have been known to become addicted to it. There are many, many good things on the Internet and many, many, many bad things on it also. You must choose to use it for the good things.

Programs

Every computer requires a program. For the computers that serve the main functions of a college, a variety of programs are available. Some will do word processing, indexing, spreadsheets, statistical functions, and so on. The list of application programs is almost without end, and people are producing more every day. No matter how sophisticated your program is, however, the quality of what comes out depends on the quality of what you put in. There is a common acronym in computer circles: GIGO—garbage in, garbage out. You can put absolute statistical trash into a statistics program, and it will perform its operations faithfully. It is up to you to know that your data are bad; your computer doesn't know that. Students sometimes use these programs without understanding what they are doing, without any sense of their appropriateness, and, worse, sometimes just on a fishing expedition in hopes that they will get the results they want.

There are programs for doing specialized accounting, programs that will give you translations, and programs for computations that mathematicians could only dream about as recently as 30 years ago. (In fact, there are entire mathematics disciplines that didn't exist before the advent of computers; fractals and chaos theory are two examples.)

Finally, you can write your own programs. If you have a talent for this, particularly if you are also good at some discipline such as microbiology, psychology, or even literature, you have an advantage. You may be able to write a program to perform some function that has hitherto been done either the long way or not at all because it was deemed impossible before computers. A word of caution: Programmers are sometimes so immersed in the process that they forget everything else. If you have an interest and a talent for programming, don't let your enthusiasm keep you from your actual study time.

Should You Buy a Computer?

The short answer is yes. Computers are becoming cheaper every day, and their power and capacity is astounding when compared to computers of just a few years ago. However, if money is tight and your college has good computer facilities, you certainly can get by without your own computer. So the long answer is, "It all depends."

If you decide to buy a laptop computer, you must have a way to keep it secure. You should probably sleep with it because laptops are very susceptible to theft. They are light and can operate for several hours at a time on their batteries. If you frequently travel home on weekends, the laptop is the only reasonable computer to have. The bigger computers with separate keyboard, monitor, CPU (the box containing the central processing unit), and printer are too cumbersome to be carrying back and forth.

Should you have your own printer? Probably. Inkjet printers are fairly cheap, but if space is at a premium (as it is in many dorms), you can do all your work on your computer and take a disk or CD to the campus computer lab to print nice-looking copy.

Handheld Calculators

You can purchase for $10 or so a calculator that science students of a generation ago would cheerfully have parted with a leg for. They can do fast, accurate calculations that used to require logarithms or a slide rule to approximate. Just because a calculator will do the heavy work in calculation, that doesn't absolve you from knowing how to do the calculations. You should know in advance what neighborhood your answer should be in. Be able to estimate an answer. Many students will accept anything their calculator tells them. Consider calculating the average age of the people living on a given block of a city. Your calculator may very well give you a display reading 27.343763489. You should understand that the only part that makes sense is 27 (or perhaps 27.3). People's ages change. That final 9 in the display probably represents tiny fractions of a second—not realistic.

For any calculator, be sure to read the manual that comes with it. Most calculators have much more capability than people realize. Some people buy a sophisticated calculator, and the only use they make of it is to balance their checkbook. All you need for that operation is a four-function calculator. Most people don't know how to use parentheses or any of the powerful mathematical functions such as powers, roots, logarithms, or the trigonometric functions.

Some calculators are very powerful indeed. They are nothing less than small computers. Some will do graphing (one by Casio will graph in three colors), some are programmable, some have complete algebra systems built in, and some can be linked to a desktop computer to share data between them. These powerful calculators are probably most useful to math and science majors. Most people need nothing more than an inexpensive scientific calculator that does almost anything an average student would require of it.

Most professors allow (or require) the use of calculators in their classes, and gear their assignments and exams to take advantage of them. Be sure that you know in advance what your teacher's policy is on the use of calculators.

Personal Digital Assistants

A fairly new device called a *personal digital assistant* (PDA) has become available in recent years. It is a very versatile tool for keeping phone numbers and addresses, scheduling time, and keeping memos. On many of them you can import photos and even play music. If you are a typical scatterbrain, you might consider buying one of these handy gadgets.

STUDYING MATHEMATICS

If you are one of those lucky students who has already successfully completed, say, intermediate algebra or trigonometry and you are not particularly stressed by the subject, then this section is not for you. But if you have not taken a math class in some time and your skills are not good (you know who you are) or if you have great fears of the subject, then we have some suggestions.

The first suggestion is to get a grip. Life doesn't stop at the door of a math classroom. You need to get a realistic assessment of your skills. Most colleges have an assessment test that will pinpoint your skill level and recommend a course to start with. Most people have an inferiority complex when it comes to math, and you may be better at it than you think. If your assessment results tell you that your greatest fear has been realized, don't despair. If you have reasonable intelligence as evidenced by good grades in English, history, and other courses, then you can do math also. The purpose of this book is not to review the entire subject. There are many books available in bookstores that do this review very well. [*How to Prepare for the ELM (the Entry Level Mathematics Test*) by Allan Mundsack is a good one.] There are three topics that often are not included in reviews of this nature that we will include here: signed numbers, the three meanings of the symbol "−," and order of operation rules.

Signed Numbers   Positive numbers are those located to the right of the zero on the number line. Negative numbers are located to the left of the zero. Zero is the only number that has no sign.

The absolute value of a number is the distance that the number is from zero on the number line. The symbol for absolute value consists of two vertical bars, one on each side of a number. For example:

$$|3| = 3$$
$$|-5| = 5$$
$$|0| = 0$$

Notice that the result of performing absolute value is always positive (or zero), never negative.

Addition

1. To add two numbers with the same sign, add their absolute values and attach the common sign to the result.

$$-5 + (-3) = -8$$
$$4 + 3 = 7$$

2. To add two numbers with different signs, *subtract* their absolute values and attach the sign of the number of the larger absolute value to the answer.

$$-9 + 3 = -6$$
$$-8 + 13 = 5$$
$$15 + (-24) = -9$$

(This rule is mistakenly memorized frequently as "subtract and take the sign of the larger." The first and third examples show why that is inadequate (3 is larger than −9, and 15 is larger than −24).

Subtraction

$$a - b = a + (-b)$$

Here's what this rule says in English: To subtract *a* minus *b*, change the operation to addition (every time) and replace the number that follows the subtraction sign by its opposite value. Then follow the rules for addition.

$$-7 - (-2) = -7 + 2 = -5$$
$$-2 - 8 = -2 + (-8) = -10$$

$$3 - (-5) = 3 + 5 = 8$$
$$-4 - (-7) = -4 + 7 = 3$$

Multiplication

To multiply two numbers, multiply their absolute values and attach a sign according to the following rules:

1. If the two numbers have the same sign, the result is positive.

2. If the two numbers have opposite signs, the result is negative.

$$(-6)(-3) = 18$$
$$5(-4) = -20$$

Division

To divide two numbers, divide their absolute values and attach a sign to the result according to the rules for multiplication.

The Three Meanings of the Symbol "–"   Many errors in mathematics occur because the symbol – is either missed or misinterpreted. One of the reasons for much of this difficulty is that there are three meanings for this symbol:

1. When the symbol "–" appears to the left of a numeral, it is read as "negative." The word negative means that the number is located to the left of zero on the number line.

$-5, -42, -\sqrt{2}, -2\frac{3}{8}$, etc.

2. When the symbol "–" appears between two numbers, it means "subtract" or "minus," and it kicks in the rule for subtraction given earlier.

$7 - (-3)$ means seven minus negative three
$-8 - 4$ means negative eight subtract four

3. When the symbol "–" appears in any other place, it should be read as "opposite" or "additive inverse." Specifically, if it is located to the left of:

a variable: $-x, -a, -t, \ldots$
parentheses: $-(x + y), -(5 - 2t), \ldots$ or
some other operation: $-2^2, -\sqrt{25}, \ldots$,

it should be read "opposite."

Order of Operation Rules

1. Do all operations inside grouping symbols first. Grouping symbols include parentheses ( ), brackets [ ], braces { }, and a bar as in $\sqrt{9 + 16}$ or $\dfrac{10 + 2}{7 - 1}$.

2. Do all roots and exponents in order from left to right.

3. Do all multiplications and divisions in order from left to right. This rule does *not* say to do all multiplications and then do all divisions—do them as you come to them in order from left to right.

4. Do all additions and subtractions (and opposites) in order from left to right. This also does not say to do all additions before subtractions—do them in order from left to right.

$$3 \cdot 2^2 = 3 \cdot 4 = 12$$
$$3 + 2(5 - 1) = 3 + 2(4) = 3 + 8 = 11$$

Another suggestion for achieving success in mathematics is to keep up with the work. Every mathematics class will be arranged sequentially, and the information is cumulative. Falling behind is the kiss of death for any math class. Form a study group early in the course and stick with it. Pick each other's brains. If you find yourself stuck at a certain point, get help immediately. You cannot afford to wait; putting it off only compounds the problem.

If you are repeating a class for some reason, maybe you failed the class before or maybe it was a long time since you had the class and you needed review, you should try to approach the class as if you had never had the class before. Start with a clean slate. Many students apply the bad habits they picked up in the previous class. If they didn't work then, they are not going to work in the new class, either.

Pick up a small chalkboard or marker board to write rules, formulas, and theorems on. Ask yourself periodically whether or not you understand what you have written on the board. Don't let anything pass you by without complete understanding.

Before you register for a math class (or any class for that matter), consult the campus grapevine. Some student organizations publish reviews of the professors on their campuses. If there isn't an official publication, many fraternities and sororities have their own lists. If all that fails, word of mouth is reliable. Talk to students who have been on campus for a year or two. Don't be shy; it's your education. Pick instructors with a good reputation among students. Some mathematics instructors are able to convey the information clearly without being intimidating or frightening. It is your job to find them.

STUDYING THE SCIENCES

As you know there are natural and social sciences. The natural sciences include physics, astronomy, chemistry, geology, and biology, all of which relate to the study nature. The social sciences include sociology, economics, and political science, which study human behavior. Psychology is both a natural science (when you study the biological aspects of human behavior) and a social science. Physical anthropology is a natural science; cultural anthropology is a social science.

Most science is inductive; that is, it begins with systematic collection of data and goes from there to summarize and interrelate those data. Some science is deductive; it begins with theories and then goes out to collect data to find out whether or not the theories are correct. Theories arrived at by either method will either be accepted or rejected according to the results of further experimentation. All stages of scientific exploration involve solving problems. Scientists must devise clever ways of collecting data. Astronomers have developed powerful telescopes and other devices for collecting data from distant objects in space. Likewise biologists have developed powerful microscopes to investigate cells and other objects too small to be seen by the naked eye. Albert Einstein developed the technique of "thought experiments" to investigate physical phenomena for which instruments have not yet been invented. Thinking up theories, refining them, and finding ways to test them also use problem-solving skills.

Mathematics is the tool that is most widely used among the sciences. Physics, engineering, and chemistry rely most heavily upon mathematics. In fact, classes in theoretical physics are also math classes at many colleges. Statistics is the primary mathematical tool that is used in sociology and social psychology. But in economics, you can expect a heavy dose of mathematics.

All sciences make use of technical language. Sometimes it is a matter of giving a highly restricted meaning to a common word. For example, in introductory physics you might learn the meaning of "force" by way of an equation: force = mass × acceleration. All the other meanings of force that you may use in your daily life are irrelevant. You must learn to forget them when you are working on physics. At other times scientists invent words to describe theories, concepts, structure, and principles. For example in atomic physics, you will learn about "quarks" and "mesons" among many other sub-atomic particles.

Scientific language is meant to be more precise than ordinary language. That is why so many strange terms are invented—to avoid confusion with ordinary meanings. Unlike ordinary words, scientific words cannot easily be learned from the context. You will be required to read and understand precise definitions of terms. Usually in scientific textbooks, technical terms are defined the first time they are used. If you somehow miss such a definition and find yourself lost, turn to the glossary. If the book doesn't have one, look in the index for the first reference to the term. The chances are good that a definition, and perhaps an example of its use, will accompany it.

Be aware, though, that knowing the definition of a scientific term is not enough—you must know how it relates to other terms and to concepts you are learning. You may begin your study of a topic by memorizing definitions of terms, but you will fully understand them only by using them and building on them as you go deeper into the subject.

The Big Three: Chemistry, Biology, and Physics

If you're reading this section of this chapter, you're likely to be taking, or thinking of taking, an introductory course in one of the three basic sciences. Although these sciences draw on one another for a complete understanding of the natural world, they differ in content and approach. We offer the following sections to point up some of these differences and give you an idea of what to expect in these college-level courses. For students who are particularly anxious about taking science classes in college, we recommend *Breaking the Science Barrier: How to Explore and Understand the Sciences* by Sheila Tobias and Carl T. Tomizuka. Students apprehensive about chemistry will find valuable tips and insights into the *process* of learning chemical material in *The Success Manual for General Chemistry* by Elizabeth Kean and Catharine Middlecamp.

Studying Chemistry   You may be studying chemistry because you intend to major in it or in a related field of science, or you may be taking it merely to satisfy the requirements of another area of study. Whatever your degree of interest in the subject, you must have heard that the introductory course in college chemistry is a killer—the course that separates the science-able from the science-hopeless. No question about it, there's a lot of complex material to learn in a short period of time. There is a lab, and there are homework assignments.

If you took chemistry in high school, you will have an easier time in college chemistry—in the beginning. But beware. Your familiarity with the terminology and the topics covered may give you a false sense of mastery, and you may find yourself lagging behind. With this in mind, we offer a few insights into studying chemistry that may help you if you are new to the subject or if you have some trepidation about taking it at all. Of course, you'll be wise to bring to the course the basic study habits and skills we presented in earlier chapters.

Although chemistry deals with "chemicals," much of chemistry is abstract. With the help of diagrams and models, you will become accustomed to thinking visually about invisible things like atoms and molecules. You will learn how chemists compress a lot of information, in very workable shorthand, into chemical formulas and reaction equations and how you can extract and make use of that information.

In chemistry you'll have to memorize certain facts, such as the symbols for the 92 naturally occurring elements. You will have to understand thoroughly a good many concepts such as molarity and reduction before you can successfully apply chemical rules and solve chemistry problems. When you study your lecture notes and read your text, it may help if you keep these categories in mind—facts, concepts, and rules. You might ask yourself, "What are the facts I need to memorize about this topic? What concepts are introduced, and how are they related to one another? Are there any rules given?" Some rules (also known as "laws" and "principles") will be stressed by your lecturer and emphasized in your text; others may not be so obvious. Be sure you understand the concepts behind the rules of chemistry. For example, Boyle's law states that the volume of a gas is inversely proportional to its pressure when the temperature and number of moles of gas are constant. Obviously, you cannot apply this law if you don't know what a mole is.

This brings us to solving chemistry problems, which can be the moment of truth as to whether or not you have mastered the material. Chemistry problems are usually stated in words, and similar types of problems may be worded differently. When you approach a problem, read it carefully and try to identify the rule or rules that apply.

It's one thing to solve a chemistry problem on a topic you're currently studying; it's another thing to solve a problem among many different types on a midterm or final exam. Our advice is to go to the exam with the basic types of problems and the steps and strategies for solving them firmly in your head. This means keeping track of the basic (generic) problems you encounter as you make your way through the course. A few days before the exam, review the list and work out as many types of problems as you can. If a problem on the exam seems unfamiliar, it may simply be a variation of one of the basic types.

Studying Biology   Biology is not considered to be as rigorous a course as chemistry, mainly because it is not problem-oriented. However, because it is in part descriptive, the vocabulary of biology is large; there are a lot of facts to memorize and a lot of concepts and processes to learn. There is chemistry involved in studying biology. Most biology courses will typically begin with atoms and molecules because these are building blocks of biological molecules as well as nonliving matter. You can learn the chemistry that pertains to biology as you go along—your textbook sets it all out—but it will be tough going without at least a high school chemistry course behind you.

Chemical reactions underlie all change within living things, and underlying all chemical reactions is energy. Cellular respiration and photosynthesis are the central energy pathways that sustain living organisms. These processes and all their ramifications are probably the hardest part for biology students to master. The Krebs cycle, with its intricate "turns," is a notorious roadblock. The diagram can be memorized, but you will not be able to follow related discussions or answer exam questions correctly unless you truly understand the steps of the cycle. But don't be discouraged by this example. In biology, perhaps more than in the other natural sciences, you can't expect to fully understand everything when it's first presented. You'll be studying topics in a particular sequence, but they won't come together until you've studied a whole unit, or even finished the course. Then all those biochemical pathways and energy transformations will link up, and the mechanisms of cellular reproduction and heredity will fall into place in the most satisfying way.

Your course in biology is likely to follow a general sequence based on levels of organization. Even if this isn't apparent, keep this concept in mind so that you'll be studying within a broad framework. You'll start with atoms and biological molecules and then go on to cells, the basic units of life, and learn how they harness energy and how they reproduce. Genes control the development of organisms; organisms form populations, communities, and ecosystems. Evolution and ecology may be unifying themes as well as separate chapters.

Somewhere toward the middle of the course, natural history will be covered—the zoology and botany you may be looking forward to. In this part of the course you will have to learn the major groups, their origins and interrelationships, their anatomies and physiologies. The organizing scheme is the system of classification created by the Swedish biologist Carolus Linnaeus in the middle of the eighteenth century, and it is still used with some modifications. The hierarchy is kingdom, phylum, class, order, family, genus, and species. Today, most biologists recognize five kingdoms; along with plants and animals are Monera (bacteria and cyanobacteria), Protista (mainly protozoans and some types of algae), and Fungi (molds and mushrooms and the like). Linnaeus's system names organisms by the binomial system: genus and species, as in *canus lupus* for wolf. You will have to memorize a certain number of these classification names.

We mention earlier that biology is not as problem-oriented as chemistry is. But in one of the subtopics of biology, genetics, you will be asked to solve problems. However the genetics problems you are likely to encounter in an introductory course are not too complicated, and they're fun to work out.

Studying Physics   The main divisions of the subject of physics are mechanics, electricity and magnetism, thermodynamics, optics, electrodynamics, relativity, quantum mechanics, and particle and nuclear physics. Physics requires memorization of fewer words by far than does geology. Behind the clearly stated laws of physics is a wide range of observations about nature, some common sense, such as Newton's first law of motion, some not, such as the theory of relativity. The basic tool of physics is measurement. There are six fundamental quantities in physics from which all other quantities can be derived. These are length (the meter), time (the second), mass (the kilogram), temperature (the kelvin), electric current (the ampere), and luminous intensity (the candela).

If the tool of physics is measurement (that produces numbers), then the language of physics is—lets face it—mathematics. In the typical physics course, equations and quantitative problems abound. The key to their solution is to apply the correct principle or law. In physics the universality of physical laws may make the task relatively easy because one law may apply to many problems. The best strategy is to reduce the problem to its essentials and consider the steps you will need to follow to get the answer. And be sure to watch your units. In every mathematical operation with measurements, the units (cm, kg, m/s^2) must be carried along with the numbers, and they must undergo the same mathematical operations as the numbers to which they are attached.

The first course you take in physics depends on your career goals and on your science and mathematical aptitude and background. Before you sign up for a course, carefully read the course description in the catalog; you can't always go by the title. "Introductory Physics" may be very different from "Introduction to Physics." Some physics classes require you to have had (or to be enrolled in) calculus; whereas others require only algebra and trigonometry. "Ideas in Physics," "Physics for Poets," and "Physics for Nonscience Majors" approach the subject intuitively with a minimum of mathematics.

Laboratory Work

Most introductory science courses have laboratories, and you may be required to take at least one during your years in college, whatever your major. Labs in different courses emphasize different skills. Usually physics labs require precise measurement; chemistry labs, careful procedures; and biology labs, detailed observation. All, however, are designed to demonstrate the scientific method—to show you firsthand how to draw inferences from observation and experimentation.

Because the kinds of experiments and observations you will do in a lab have been done by thousands, indeed millions, of students before, there is a tendency to regard them as mechanical chores to be gotten through as painlessly as possible. Avoid that view. Many of the experiments you will do are repetitions of discoveries of fundamental scientific principles. Try to put yourself in the position of the people who first made those discoveries.

You should be careful, accurate, and complete in keeping records of your measurements and data. Check all calculations. If you have a workbook, keep it neat. Scientists are neat at least about their science, and a sloppy workbook is not going to make a good impression on your lab instructor. You will be given a set of procedures for reporting the results of your experiments that you must follow strictly. Scientists set great store in orderly procedures, and if you follow the rules both in conducting the experiments and in reporting them, you will be getting into the habitual ways of doing things in that particular science.

Reading Science Texts

In Chapter 4 we say that different subjects require different strategies in reading. In this section we say a few things about reading science texts.

Problems   In scientific texts, examples and problems are worked out for you in the text itself. Don't just read these. Even if you think you understand, if you read without a pencil, you may skip over some crucial step that you really don't follow. Work through each problem yourself just as it is presented in the text. That way you will really know if you can do each step. If you can get the same answer at each step as the answer given in the textbook, the chances are that you know how to do all the operations. Occasionally in texts in the physical sciences and engineering, the obvious steps in some mathematical derivation are skipped. But when you try to do the derivation or solve the problem, don't skip steps. Make sure that you know all the intervening steps that the author did not include.

Graphs and Diagrams   Scientific texts are full of graphs and diagrams. These aren't just decorative devices used to break up pages of solid print. They are essential to an understanding of the text. Be sure to read them and make sure that you understand every aspect of them.

Graphs are among the most common illustrations found in scientific texts. Most graphs illustrate a mathematical relationship between two variables. A line, such as a curve, will give you a visual interpretation of some observational phenomenon which may or may not correspond to an algebraic equation. One of the tasks of scientists is to determine whether or not there is a mathematical equation that adequately describes the results of observations. The process of finding such an equation is called "curve fitting." Some observed data lie on a line; the relationship is linear. The observed points of data for some other experiment might lie most nearly on the graph of a parabola in which case a quadratic equation might be used to describe the phenomenon. Other data may not obviously fit any algebraic relationship.

One of the most elementary experiments in physics is to measure the distance a steel ball travels in regularly timed intervals when it rolls down an inclined plane. If the times are measured along the horizontal scale on a graph and the corresponding distances along the vertical scale, you will find that the distances vary in proportion to the square of the time traveled. The graph would resemble the graph of $y = 2 + 0.5x^2$ in the diagram for Reading a Graph on page 179.

Not all diagrams are graphs. Sometimes information can be conveyed most conveniently by means of a pie chart (budgets are particularly well suited to a pie chart), a bar chart, a pictogram, a scatter diagram, or another device. Sometimes a photograph (especially in biology) is the best means of illustrating a concept. Whatever graph or diagram is used, you should study it. Make sure you understand the concept behind the diagram. Often it is a good idea to sketch out the diagram yourself to make sure you understand it. Whether a diagram is provided in the text or one you have drawn yourself,

Reading a Graph

Each line represents an equation on two variables, x and y. For any given equation, you can find the value of y that corresponds to given value of x. The straight line represents the equation $y = 0 + 0.5x$, and the curved line represents the equation $y = 2 + 0.5x^2$.

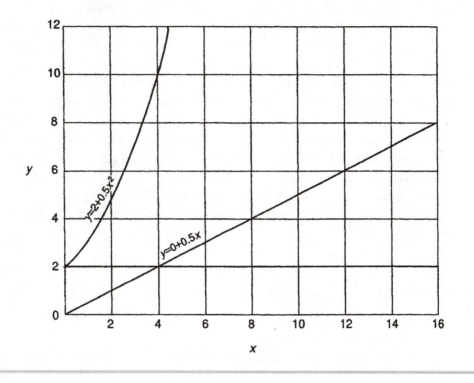

it should help you to conceptualize and remember essential information such as the relation between population and birth rate or the parts of a flower.

Tables   Students sometimes skip tables because they find them dull, detailed, and hard to read. Don't skip them. The information in a table is important. At the very least make sure you understand *the principle by which the table is organized*. Sometimes a table will give the same information that might be given in a graph.

The Metric System

The United States is, regrettably, one of the few nations on Earth that does not consistently use the metric system for measurement. We in America are still hampered by things being measured in feet, yards, miles, quarts, gallons, bushels, pecks, hogsheads (for crying out loud!), ounces, pounds, tons, and myriad others for which you have to remember numbers such as 12, 3, 16, 4, 5280, 63 (!), 8, 32, and 2000 to navigate from one unit to another. The metric system is a very simple system whose basic measurements are the meter, the gram, and the liter, as well as the second, and the only number you need for navigation is 10. The metric system is a decimal system, and since we do calculations with decimal numbers all the time, it would be much, much more convenient if all our measurements were in a decimal system to begin with. Then conversions between units of measure would be a matter of moving a decimal point around. For example, 253 cm is equivalent to 2.53 m. (Compare the similar problem of converting 253 inches to feet. You have to divide by 12 to get $21\frac{1}{12}$ feet or 12 feet 1 inch.) Also 253 cg is equivalent to 2.53 g just as easily. The following device can be used to easily navigate in the metric system.

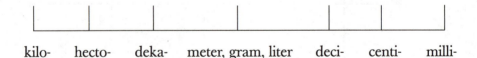

kilo-   hecto-   deka-   meter, gram, liter   deci-   centi-   milli-

To convert a measurement from, say, centimeters (cm) to meters (m), count the number of spaces on the diagram from "centi-" to "meters." Then move the decimal point the same number of places in the same direction—two places to the left. To convert 0.0024 km to cm, count five spaces to the right from "kilo-" to "centi-" and move the decimal point five places to the right. So 0.0024 km is equivalent to 240 cm. (Consider the similar task of converting $\frac{3}{16}$ of a mile to inches, and you will soon see the benefit of the metric system.)

Most people's apprehension about the metric system is the worry of converting pounds to kilograms, for example, or inches to centimeters or gallons to liters. Such conversions are almost never necessary. Once you get familiar with measuring things in metric units, why would you want to know what the corresponding measurement is in the U.S. system? You will be accustomed to saying, "It's about 3 kilometers to school," or "I am about 183 centimeters tall," or "I weigh about 77 kilograms." You will still be able to say, "A

Converting to the Metric System

Here are the metric equivalents of some of the more common U.S. units.

1 inch	= 2.5400 centimeters	1 centimeter	= 0.3937 inch
1 foot	= 0.3048 meter	1 meter	= 3.2808 feet
1 yard	= 0.9144 meter	1 meter	= 1.0936 yards
1 mile	= 1.6093 kilometers	1 kilometer	= 0.6214 mile
1 quart	= 0.9464 liter	1 liter	= 1.0567 quarts
1 gallon	= 3.7854 liters	1 liter	= 0.2642 gallon
1 ounce	= 28.3495 grams	1 gram	= 0.0353 ounce
1 pound	= 0.4536 kilogram	1 kilogram	= 2.2046 pounds

miss is as good as a mile," and the game of football will not change. We have provided a table of equivalent measures in metric units and U.S. units, but it is more a matter of interest than necessity. (See above.)

A CONCLUDING WORD

We have touched on only the most elementary aspects of science and math. If you are one of the many people who has been labeled "dumb in math" or "having no head for science," you don't have to resign yourself to accepting those labels as your destiny. You have just missed out on something. You don't have to be illiterate in math and science. If necessary, get someone to help you. Many colleges and universities run special remedial programs in math. If you are deficient and your institution has such a program, the sooner you take advantage of it the better. It may be to your advantage to attend a local community college to take the remedial classes you need. Besides being less expensive, you will most likely find that they are better prepared to deal with students who are lacking in the basics.

Math anxiety is a curable problem. Many colleges have periodic math anxiety clinics with the purpose of helping students relax and be able to learn without the burden of the dread many people have for the subject. Because of the consequences to your academic career, you should do something to alleviate your phobia as soon as possible.

Getting Help

We have tried to show you how to become a better student by improving your classroom skills and learning how to study textbooks and write papers more effectively. There are many other resources, some of which may be pointed out at orientation, some of which will be suggested by your instructors, and some of which you will have to ferret out on your own. Furthermore, there are things you can do to improve the quality of your life as a student. Leading a happy and fulfilling life is an important ingredient in getting the most out of your 4 years (or so) as a college student.

USING STUDY AIDS EFFECTIVELY

Workbooks and Study Guides

Workbooks and study guides, often combined in a single volume, sometimes go along with textbooks assigned in college courses. Many textbooks have specific software that is designed to assist students. Some even have a CD version of the textbook itself. These supplementary items usually include special projects and exercises that illustrate and explain the textbook along with review questions and self-test items that provide practice for examinations.

Some instructors will require the workbook; others may recommend it but not require it. Even if your instructor does not mention a workbook or other supplement at all, you should find out whether one does accompany your textbook. Ancillary materials for students are usually mentioned in the preface to the textbook. If it's not there, try the back cover—it may be listed there as advertising blurb for your textbook. You might even try calling the publisher of your book. They will know for sure what is available. Almost all supplements are of some value, and some will give you a lot of help.

Outside Readings

Textbooks usually make up most of the reading for introductory courses. In more advanced courses and in some introductory courses, instructors assign or recommend outside readings. Too many students ignore such readings. Those students are not likely to be the ones who earn top grades but are the ones who merely try to get by. That's too bad because outside readings give depth to one's education. For one thing, they will help you understand the textbook. For another, they will give you a different perspective on the subject. Conscientious instructors, who know that everyone has biases, often assign outside readings that take a different point of view from the one in the textbook. In the humanities, outside readings provide the real essentials. To read about Plato in a textbook on the history of philosophy is only an introduction to Plato himself. Finally, outside readings can make study more satisfying and arouse your curiosity. Often it is the outside readings that spark a deep interest in the subject matter. They may even lead you to the choice of a major.

Journals and periodicals of all kinds provide another perspective for your education. Textbooks, even those with a recent copyright date, are sometimes out of date. Journals and periodicals can fill in the recent details on a subject. Aside from technical journals that probably won't interest you unless you are doing research in a particular field, there are many periodicals and newspapers that can provide anyone with the background for a good education. Reading widely among the journals and periodicals is a good way to develop your own personal philosophy. You will agree with some writers and disagree with others while forming opinions of your own. Try some of the reliable standbys such as *The Wall Street Journal, Business Week, The Economist, Harpers, The Atlantic Monthly, The New York Review of Books,* and *The American Spectator.* For variety and a different perspective try *The Utne Reader* or *Alibi.*

There are periodicals also for every personal interest and craft from knitting and antiquing to woodworking and motorcycles. There are popular magazines with excellent photography and interesting articles of current culture such as *Smithsonian* and *National Geographic*. As a student, you should develop the habit of reading—read constantly; read voraciously. Find a couple of your favorite periodicals and subscribe to them. That way not only will you have a constant source of material to read, but you will also be promoting the type of writing that you find most interesting and rewarding.

You should read a newspaper every day. Sure, read the comics and the sports pages if that's your interest, but read everything on the front page. And the opinion page and the op ed page are musts. Keep in touch with the world even when you are immersed in study. Have something to talk about when you have a moment to relax.

Find the general periodical room of your library and look through what it has to offer. Even a modest library will provide an astounding range of features of modern intellectual life. It is the good students who make use of such facilities. But how can you become interested if you don't know about them?

Films, Videos, and TV Instruction

Films and videotapes are often used as teaching aids. When they are done well, they combine the best features of an instructor's explanation with the visual presentation that cannot be brought into the classroom in any other way. Such films and tapes are often entertaining, and therein lies a problem. Students sit back and relax during the film, or even go to sleep. But if the film is doing its job, it has to be studied as carefully as a textbook or class notes. Pay attention to what the instructor says about the film. Take notes if you can. Look for the main ideas. Because a film moves fast, it is important that you jot down all the main points as soon as the film is over, or you will forget them.

At many colleges and universities, entire courses are broadcast over public TV channels. One of the big advantages of courses taught in this manner is that you can tape them and play them at more convenient times. They are usually broadcast during early morning hours for this reason—they expect you to tape the shows. But once the shows are on tape, you can also play them over and over again for review. You may not like the idea of not being able to ask questions, but there is usually an instructor assigned to such courses who can be contacted either by phone or e-mail to answer questions. Televised courses are a good way to take a few extra units by utilizing some extra time you might have.

More and more courses are being offered entirely over the Internet. The instruction is conducted entirely by a program that guides you through the material at your own pace and records both the time you spend working on the course and your scores on tests. There are some hybrid courses of this type during which you must meet with an instructor at a certain time and location for exams, but all other time spent on the course is at your discretion.

Be on the lookout for other innovative methods of instruction that may arise because of burgeoning computer development.

GETTING HELP FROM SPECIAL SOURCES

There are times when everyone needs help from other people. In college, academic advising is routine. Every college or university provides assistance on a more personal level also. The various services that exist for your benefit often mean the difference between academic success and failure, not to mention the difference between being miserable and being happy.

Academic Advising

Every school has its own system for helping students choose courses and decide on a major. In many places, every student is assigned a faculty adviser. The adviser's duty is to help the student in all matters academic. In other institutions advisers are located in a counseling office, and the counselors usually have other duties besides academic advising—matriculation and orientation, for example. How the relationship works in practice between you and your adviser depends on how well the two of you hit it off.

First of all, do for yourself all that you can do. Read the catalog and the various books and handouts provided to students. Consult the schedule of classes. Do the arithmetic to determine how many credits you will need to complete each semester or quarter. When you have worked out a tentative schedule and thought about any questions you have, see your adviser. The adviser's job is to advise, not to make your decisions for you. Your adviser may be able to give you information you can't get for yourself and offer opinions based on a lot of experience. But the decisions are yours. If you don't get along well with your adviser, seek help from an academic dean. Your adviser is the first place to go for answers to questions you can't get from the college catalog or other officially printed material. Don't rely on the student grapevine for crucial information.

Suppose you are working hard in one of your courses, but you just can't seem to master the material. What should you do? The first thing is to face your problem as soon as possible. Don't drift along hoping that things will take care of themselves. Don't wait for an F on a midterm to tell you what you probably knew all along. As soon as you sense difficulties, ask yourself the following questions: "Am I adequately prepared for this course? Do other students have background that I lack? Is there some single thing that gives me trouble? Do I understand the terminology? Do I have trouble doing calculations, problems, or lab work? Am I swamped by the reading?"

The next step is to decide whether or not you can do something about your problem or whether you should drop the course. You need advice. Confer with your instructor. You may have inadvertently gotten yourself into a course that is too advanced for you. This happens often in foreign languages and mathematics, especially if you thought you had the prerequisites in high school or another institution.

It is not a good idea to drop a class impulsively without seeking the advice of your instructor, adviser, or dean. This is particularly true if the course is required either for your major or for graduation. Many colleges ask that students get approval from both the instructor and the adviser to drop a course just to ensure that the student is taking a wise action.

If you have waited too long to drop a course without some sort of penalty, it is still not too late to confer with the instructor to see what is possible to remedy the situation. Most instructors are willing to show you the source of your errors, what you did wrong on exams, and what you might do to pull out of a dismal spot. Of course, there may be nothing you can do to avoid a failing grade. Even so, you should have learned something about how to avoid similar difficulties in the future. A grade of F is not the end of your academic world—view it as a warning signal.

Counseling Services

Personal problems often get in the way of academic work. If you have personal worries or difficulties that make it hard for you to work, you ought to be able to tell these problems to your adviser and ask for help or guidance. Often just the act of telling someone else will make it better, or perhaps your adviser can offer a word of wisdom. If the problem doesn't seem to have an immediate solution, your adviser may be able to refer you to a counseling center or to a qualified professional counselor in the community.

Your counseling services are especially prepared to deal with the typical problems of students. Conflict with parents, feelings of insecurity, problems with roommates or others, sexual problems, inability to concentrate, and myriad other problems are the sort of things they deal with every day. If one of these problems is hampering your performance in school, get help.

Medical Services

The years in college are not the healthiest of a person's life. Poor eating habits, insufficient sleep, and crowded and badly ventilated classrooms all contribute to a lowered resistance to infection. Mononucleosis, flu, and other respiratory diseases are endemic on campuses. Students are constantly warned about the entire set of sexually transmitted diseases. You must take these warnings seriously—some of these diseases will follow you around for the rest of your life. And you know that HIV-AIDS has even more serious consequences. If you even *suspect* that you have a sexually transmitted disease, make it your first priority to consult your medical services.

If you are sexually active, visit your local Planned Parenthood office or your doctor. Babies, while cute, are *very* inconvenient for students. "Safe sex" is not just a motto; it's required, and if your partner is not willing to take precautions, then it is up to you. If, despite your best efforts at contraception, you find yourself pregnant, you have some decisions to make as soon as possible. Your baby needs to have proper prenatal care. (These last few sentences are directed to men as well as women—they apply to both of you.) Again, this would be the time to see your doctor or Planned Parenthood.

Tutorial and Remedial Services

If you are having trouble in a particular course, you can easily find someone to tutor you for a fee. This can be very effective, especially if you need help over one troublesome part of the class. Many colleges maintain tutoring services that are free for students' use. These services are staffed by advanced undergraduates or graduate students. Tutoring is usually available in the "hard" subjects such as mathematics, chemistry, biology, physics, and foreign languages.

Some instructors schedule optional special sessions for students who think they might be in trouble. These sessions are usually scheduled in the evening or on weekends. Too often the students who show up are the ones who need it least. If you find work in some classes difficult, be sure to go to every extra-help session offered even if you have to give up something else.

We mentioned earlier that a well-functioning study group can be very beneficial. In addition to picking each other's brains, the best way to understand anything is to explain it to someone else. We always recommend that if you have the opportunity to tutor, take it. You will learn much more than the person you are tutoring.

Many four-year colleges and universities admit students who are deficient in certain subjects, such as English and math, with the understanding that they have a certain amount of time to boost their skills to an acceptable level. Community colleges provide a wide range of remedial courses at a much lower cost than university courses. These courses are not transferable, but they bring students up to the level necessary for college work. Some students take courses at both the university and the community college at the same time while bringing up their abilities.

The story of Joe is typical among community college students. Joe was one of seven children in a poor family. Almost everyone in his town was an immigrant or first-generation American with a blue-collar job. His father was an unskilled worker, and he died when Joe was 10. Joe liked school and did well, but when he was in eighth grade, the school counselor advised him to enter a vocational program in high school. Joe made it through high school and got a job as a mechanic in a neighborhood garage after he graduated. He was good at his work, and one day one of his customers remarked. "Joe, you're smart. You should be an engineer or something."

This casual remark set him thinking. He went to the public library, and, with the help of the librarian, found some books and pamphlets about various careers in engineering. His interest was piqued, and the librarian suggested that he talk to someone at the local community college. The result was that 2 years after his graduation from high school, Joe entered college as a part-time student while he continued to work at his mechanics job.

He was insecure, and the work was harder and more theoretical than he thought it would be. Fortunately, his community college was equipped to deal with Joe's unique needs. He took three remedial courses in his first year: one in mathematics, one in reading, and one in English composition. By the end of his second year, he had earned a B in chemistry and an A in calculus. At the end of his third year, he applied for admission to the school of engineering at the state university. He was accepted.

But his troubles only began. He was away from home for the first time, and he had to borrow money to make a go of it. After living all his life in the small town, he was in an unfamiliar cosmopolitan environment. What is more, he was taking upper-division classes for the first time, and they nearly did him in.

He brought his problems to his adviser who suggested that Joe take advantage of a new tutorial program set up by the engineering school. The result was that his first-semester grades were okay, and his second-semester grades were good. Two years later, Joe received his bachelor's degree in electrical engineering.

Many students have stories like Joe's. Community colleges serve many people as the last resort. Without their many services with remedial courses, students with Joe's potential would have no chance.

Career Counseling

Many people enter college with firm intentions about their career, and, after a semester or two, they discover that they really have a passion for some other career completely. College is the time for experimenting with different classes, and we recommend keeping an open mind about career choices. Ulcers are born in careers where you hate to go to work every day, and this stems from your making the wrong choice in college.

Most colleges maintain an office devoted to career planning and placement. This office is for freshmen who have no idea how to focus their interests as well as for seniors who know what they want to do but need a job. The freshmen need to assess their abilities, interests, values, priorities, and goals; whereas the seniors need to know how to prepare résumés and how to do well at job interviews. Students who intend to go to graduate or professional school need to know what the admission requirements are and how to apply.

One of the services provided by the career planning and placement office is to keep a file for you in which you can place letters of recommendation from professors or deans. This file will be kept for many years after graduation so that, even 10 years later, it may be sent to a new prospective employer.

Consider the case of Jill. Jill entered her state university with the intention of becoming a doctor. She took the basic premed chemistry course in her freshman year, and, although she did well enough in it, she didn't really like it. She discovered the intellectual excitement of studying philosophy, and she enjoyed her literature and history classes. She finally decided to leave the sciences and concentrate on the humanities with a major in history.

Jill assumed that after graduation she would probably go to law school because she had heard that law schools had no specific course requirements other than a background in the liberal arts, high grades, and good LSAT scores. When she reached her senior year, however, she knew that she didn't want to go to law school. She graduated with high honors, took a civil service exam, and got a job in the planning office of the suburban county where she had grown up. The job interested her, and, after 2 years, she applied for graduate work in architecture. She had a talent for it, and, in the summers, she worked in a prestigious firm of city planners. When she got through her architecture school, she landed a job in the firm, an occupation she really likes.

The point of Jill's story is that as a freshman, you really don't know what you want to do. It is good to have plans, but you must be willing to change your plans when circumstances develop in a different direction. If you have an excellent academic record in your major, you have many options open to you, even outside your major field. Your job as a student is to do the very best you can in each of your classes so that your cumulative record will impress graduate schools and employers alike. Keep all your options open.

If you completely screw up and drop out with a dismal record, the best plan might be to work for a year or two to gain a little more maturity and then start again at a community college where you can regroup and recoup. Many students find a second chance at their local community college, discover their true interest, and transfer to the university. Studies have shown that students who transfer from a community college have better grade point averages at the university than students who went straight to the university out of high school.

Older Students in College

There was a time when everyone in college was between the ages of 17 and 22, but beginning after World War II, the average age of college students has risen until now it is about 30. Many women, who took time out to raise a family, returned to college to complete their education after their children had grown. People who had either been laid off from their work or who decided to make a career change returned to college to gain the skills necessary to find a new job.

If you are an older student returning to college, you have one big advantage over the other students—maturity. You have already solved many of the problems that plague younger people. This leaves you free to apply your energy to your academic pursuit without those annoyances.

Older students frequently have great anxiety about returning to school after many years because they think they have lost their academic skills, and they can't compete with the sharp, younger minds. The evidence is that older students make better grades than their counterparts even when they have to hold down a job or when they have small children at home.

Many colleges have special programs designed for working adults in which students attend one or two evenings each week and Saturdays. People with jobs and a family find it takes many years (maybe 10 to 15 years) to graduate; whereas other full-time students usually graduate in 4 years. These special programs allow even working adults to graduate in about 5 years. One such program is the Program for Accelerated College Education (PACE) that is becoming more and more popular across the country as its success becomes well known. Originating at Wayne State University in Detroit, PACE has proliferated among community colleges across the country. At every school where PACE exists, it is becoming clear that the program is a great success, and that the top students of each graduating class are likely to be PACE students.

Flora Wilson had 2 years at a top women's college 30 years ago. She married at the end of her second year, and she settled into being a full-time homemaker, caring for her four children. Through PTA activities, she got interested in community affairs, and by the time her last child was in high school, she was a respected civic leader with an important role in local and state politics. Despite her success, she felt self-conscious about her lack of a college degree. After a lot of thought and uncertainty and with plenty of encouragement from her friends, she returned to college. Well into her fifties, she was accepted into a very strong local university, and she was able to get nearly all of her earlier credits transferred. She worked a little harder at first than she needed to, but she enjoyed it, and she got to know a lot of young people, some of whom came to visit her at her home regularly. When she graduated after 2 years, she promptly got a job on the staff of an important local politician, and she is thoroughly engrossed in her work.

Betty Little got married before she even finished high school. She and her husband had three children. With great effort, she was able to work part time and take care of the children while her husband finished his education. When he got his bachelor's degree, he said, "Betty, now it's your turn." She made up her high school deficiencies and enrolled in a nearby university as a freshman. She was 28 with three children under the age of 10. It wasn't easy for her; the demands on her time were horrendous, but she was well organized, and, above all, she liked being in college. As soon as she got her degree, her husband started work on a Ph.D. in education.

When their children were grown up, Nick and Joni both decided to go back to school. After taking the assessment tests at a local community college, they found that they both needed some remedial work in English and math, and they enrolled in the PACE program at their college. During their first semester, they found other students with similar backgrounds and interests and formed a study group that met regularly at one or another of the members' homes. This group remained together for 3 years, and through mutual support and assistance, the entire group graduated. Then Nick and Joni both enrolled in the PACE program at the local university where they formed another study group and eventually graduated with bachelor's degrees. All this happened, mind you, while they both continued to work full time. Joni has subsequently enrolled in a graduate program at the university, and Nick is now working at the university with plans to get a graduate degree also and return to the community college where it all began to teach.

These examples are typical of the experiences of older students. Do they have problems? Of course, but not insurmountable ones. If you have the desire for a college education after being away from it for a while, you have options available. You should investigate the programs provided by your local colleges for students in your circumstances. Most likely, there is a way it can be done.

MAKING A GOOD PERSONAL ADJUSTMENT

The college years are a transitional period in a person's life. As students make new academic and personal adjustments, they are aware that in a short time they will be on their own. The world outside the academic walls can seem threatening. Getting that first job after graduation, finding a place to live, making all sorts of decisions that will affect professional and personal lives, each student will have no lack of things to worry about.

Though you will probably look back on your college years with nostalgia, you may also find the period to be full of stress. There is no simple formula for getting you through the adjustment problems you may have, but there are some good principles, most of them common sense, that may help you.

1. Be realistic. Well-adjusted people are realistic about most things. They know what they want, they set reasonable goals for themselves, and they know how to avoid trouble. Find out what you can reasonably expect to achieve and adjust your efforts and goals accordingly. Don't underestimate yourself. If you get mediocre grades, find out why. Are you bored? Do you lack the right background? Are you studying the wrong things?

Don't overestimate yourself. For example, you might want to question your goal of becoming a doctor if you can't make it through chemistry and your work habits are less than excellent. You would also want to think about how much money a medical education is going to cost. The point is to be realistic and know yourself and your circumstances. Take Forrest, for example:

When Forrest was accepted into a prestigious university, he intended to be a doctor, and he wanted to do all the extracurricular things as well. Soon after he entered, he joined the local symphony orchestra, and he got involved with student politics. But he didn't like his studies; he didn't work hard enough academically to meet his ambitions. He dropped out of school, became a jazz musician (his classical background helped out), and, in his midtwenties, he had a successful career with his own band. He may someday want to go back to school, but probably not in medicine.

Face your personal problems as objectively as you can, but sometimes your friends can be more objective than you can be. That's what friends are for, but don't put them on the spot. They may not want to hurt your feelings. If friends can't help, try your adviser. Most colleges are full of groups that offer peer counseling about special problems such as sex or drugs. A peer counselor is another student who can be more objective about your problems than either you or your friends can be.

2. *Accept anxiety*. Some anxiety is a good thing. If you didn't have a little anxiety about your exams, you probably wouldn't prepare for them as well as you should. Most circumstances that cause anxiety turn out not to be as bad as our imagination leads us to believe, and anxiety dissipates.

Sometimes, however, anxiety becomes unreasonable. If that happens to you, you should be concerned. If you feel very anxious and can't attribute it to any particular thing but it seems to invade your whole life, then you need to do something about it. Common refuges such as drugs, alcohol, or immersion in TV will not help.

3. *Don't be defensive*. When we have anxiety and no way of doing something about it, we try to fool ourselves in various ways. You might say, for example, that the exam you failed was unfair, that the instructor misled you about what to prepare for. This takes the blame away from you and externalizes it.

There are a number of ways of externalizing things as a defense against anxiety. Psychologists call these defense mechanisms because what they do is defend our egos from anxiety, fear of failure, and feelings of personal inadequacy. Defense mechanisms are often harmless and convenient ways of making us feel better about the bad things that happen to us. But if they become a substitute for working to eliminate the source of our difficulties and are used to sidestep persistent and severe problems, they can be a source of real trouble.

Finally, our defenses have a way of breaking down under severe stress with the result that we are suddenly flooded with feelings of anxiety or depression. These feelings are not only uncomfortable, but they can totally incapacitate a person.

4. Understand what you want and set goals. Defenses are sometimes ways of fooling yourself about your own motives. When your grades are poor, it is easy to blame everyone or everything but yourself—your instructor, a bad cold, family problems, etc. You might see that while, sure, you want good grades, you really *don't* want to work for them. It's hard to be the sparkling center of the social scene of your fraternity or sorority and at the same time make the grades to get into Harvard Law School. You can't have everything you want, and rather than let circumstances decide what you get, decide for yourself.

5. Alter goals appropriately. Fred came to college with the idea of being a doctor only to be frustrated by his lack of interest in the premed courses. In the middle of his second year, his anxiety about the difficulties he experienced in chemistry reached an acute state. He sought help at the counseling center, where, after a few sessions, he acknowledged that medicine was a goal his family had set for him, and being a doctor was not what he wanted for himself. He realized that his poor performance was in part a rebellion against parental pressure. Though he had to face his disappointed parents, he set career goals toward things that were closer to his own interests and abilities.

6. Learn to postpone satisfactions. When two motives conflict, one way to resolve the conflict is to postpone the satisfaction of one of them. This is a way of taking control of your life rather than letting circumstances and other people control it for you. Most college students know that, but sometimes they don't practice it on a regular basis. If you are going to participate in student government or work on the student paper, you will have to postpone something else to make time. Or maybe it's the other way around. You may have to drop off the student paper because it takes too much time from something else. The point is, examine your options and choose one. If you don't, circumstances may choose worse for you.

7. *Keep busy.* Keeping occupied with useful things is another mark of a well-adjusted person. This doesn't mean you should forever be running around frantically doing things; what it means is doing things so that you have some sense of accomplishment. It may also mean doing enough to keep yourself from dwelling on your troubles or from resorting to alcohol or drugs. Work is not a cure for emotional problems, but it often keeps us from making those problems worse, and, in the long run, it may provide some deep satisfaction.

All this may sound a little old-fashioned in an age in which we are supposed to be free to do whatever we want. But the idea that we are completely free to do whatever is in our power is a delusion. The minute we decide to do one thing, it becomes impossible to do something else. If you are going to master organic chemistry, you can't spend every evening drinking yourself silly. If you don't recognize your own real self—your goals, aspirations, prejudices, sexual feelings, emotions, abilities—you will end up being victimized by your ignorance.

If you are very mixed up, reading this or any other book will not help much. You need to explore your problems with the kind of give-and-take that occurs in a personal or group counseling situation. It doesn't matter so much what the setting is—health services, a psychological clinic, or your doctor's office—as it does that you recognize that you have a problem that you can't solve on your own.

College isn't training for life; it is life. This book is mostly about coping with the intellectual demands of college because these are the central purposes of college. You can't meet those demands unless you have both the skills to apply them and the personal adjustment to free yourself to do so.

Provisional Working Schedule

Time \ Day	Monday	Tuesday	Wednesday	Thursday	Friday	Saturday	Sunday
7:00 a.m.							
8:00							
8:30							
9:00							
9:30							
10:00							
10:30							
11:00							
11:30							
12:00							
12:30 p.m.							
1:00							
1:30							
2:00							
2:30							
3:00							
3:30							
4:00							
4:30							
5:00							
5:30							
6:00							
6:30							
7:00							
7:30							
8:00							
8:30							
9:00							
9:30							
10:00							
10:30							
11:00							

Provisional Working Schedule

Time \ Day	Monday	Tuesday	Wednesday	Thursday	Friday	Saturday	Sunday
7:00 a.m.							
8:00							
8:30							
9:00							
9:30							
10:00							
10:30							
11:00							
11:30							
12:00							
12:30 p.m.							
1:00							
1:30							
2:00							
2:30							
3:00							
3:30							
4:00							
4:30							
5:00							
5:30							
6:00							
6:30							
7:00							
7:30							
8:00							
8:30							
9:00							
9:30							
10:00							
10:30							
11:00							

Final Working Schedule

Time / Day	Monday	Tuesday	Wednesday	Thursday	Friday	Saturday	Sunday
7:00 a.m.							
8:00							
8:30							
9:00							
9:30							
10:00							
10:30							
11:00							
11:30							
12:00							
12:30 p.m.							
1:00							
1:30							
2:00							
2:30							
3:00							
3:30							
4:00							
4:30							
5:00							
5:30							
6:00							
6:30							
7:00							
7:30							
8:00							
8:30							
9:00							
9:30							
10:00							
10:30							
11:00							

Final Working Schedule

Time \ Day	Monday	Tuesday	Wednesday	Thursday	Friday	Saturday	Sunday
7:00 a.m.							
8:00							
8:30							
9:00							
9:30							
10:00							
10:30							
11:00							
11:30							
12:00							
12:30 p.m.							
1:00							
1:30							
2:00							
2:30							
3:00							
3:30							
4:00							
4:30							
5:00							
5:30							
6:00							
6:30							
7:00							
7:30							
8:00							
8:30							
9:00							
9:30							
10:00							
10:30							
11:00							

Weekly Schedule

	Monday	Tuesday	Wednesday	Thursday	Friday	Saturday	Sunday
1 am							
2 am							
3 am							
4 am							
5 am							
6 am							
7 am							
8 am							
9 am							
10 am							
11 am							
12 noon							
1 pm							
2 pm							
3 pm							
4 pm							
5 pm							
6 pm							
7 pm							
8 pm							
9 pm							
10 pm							
11 pm							
12 midnt							

Index

Locators in **bold** indicate illustrative material